CROCK·POT

• THE ORIGINAL SLOW COOKER •

GLUTEN-FREE
Recipes

Publications International, Ltd.

Pictured on the front cover: Seafood Stew *(page 42).*

Pictured on the back cover *(clockwise from top):* Curry Chicken with Peaches and Raisins *(page 66),* Horseradish Roast Beef and Potatoes *(page 192)* and Lemon and Tangerine Glazed Carrots *(page 163).*

ISBN-13: 978-1-4508-7051-1
ISBN-10: 1-4508-7051-1

Library of Congress Control Number: 2013932210

Manufactured in China.

8 7 6 5 4 3 2 1

Contents

Introduction

Gluten-Free Living

What is gluten anyway? It's not just wheat. Gluten is a protein that is found naturally in wheat, rye, and barley. Gluten gives structure to the baked goods we know and love. Without it, or something to replace it, bread and cake would be sad little puddles or piles of crumbs. When yeast, baking powder, or other leavening agents produce bubbles in a dough or a batter, that air is trapped by the stretchy gluten network and the baked product rises and becomes light.

Legend has it that gluten was discovered by 7th century Buddhist monks who were trying to find something to replace the texture and savor of meat in their vegetarian diets. They found that when they submerged dough made with wheat flour in water, the starch washed away. What was left behind was a gummy mass with an almost meatlike texture—gluten. Today gluten is still used to make seitan, mock duck and other meat replacement products.

Millions of Americans are going gluten-free for dozens of reasons. Some have been told that they must by their doctors. Others just feel better when they stop eating gluten. Some parents feel that a gluten-free diet improves the behavior patterns of their children, including those with ADHD and autism. And there are those who just think it's trendy. Truth is, if giving up gluten didn't improve so many lives, people wouldn't be willing to make the effort. There is one caveat: if you want to try gluten-free living but haven't been tested for celiac disease, you need to be tested BEFORE you start the diet. Otherwise test results will be meaningless.

Going gluten-free means you may have to start bringing a magnifying glass on your shopping trips. At the very least, you will learn a great deal about the many ingredients that go into all the processed food most of us take for granted. You may even decide that paying attention to the ingredients list is a lot more relevant than some of the marketing hype that appears on the front of the package.

The red flag you're searching for is the word "wheat." If anything in the product contains, or is made from wheat, by law it must be listed as such. Next, look for any ingredients you don't recognize. Chances are you'll find a few multisyllabic words that sound like they came from the chemistry lab. You'll need to check a list of safe and unsafe ingredients to figure those out. (You can even download such lists for your smart phone these days. See **www.celiac.com** for information.)

Soon enough, you'll recognize the most common ones that can be a problem (even if you never do learn how to pronounce them).

THE SHORT LIST

**Sensitivities differ from person to person and ingredients
differ from brand to brand. Always check the label's fine print.
This is an abbreviated list of some of the most commonly used items.**

RED LIGHTS: (contain gluten)

barley	couscous	imitation seafood	pretzels
beer	durum	kamut	rye
bran	einkorn	malt vinegar	seitan
brewer's yeast	emmer	malt, malt flavoring,	semolina
bulgur	graham	malt extract	spelt
cereal	gravies and sauces	matzo	tabbouleh
commercial baked goods	groats (barley or wheat)	orzo	wheat
	hydrolyzed wheat protein	pizza	

Yellow Lights: (may contain gluten)

artificial color*	emulsifiers	marinades	pasta sauce
baking powder	flavorings	modified food starch*	salad dressings
barbecue sauce	frozen vegetables with sauce/seasonings	mustard	soba noodles
caramel color*		nondairy creamer	soy sauce
dextrins*	hydrolyzed plant protein (HPP)	oats	vegetable broth

These items are gluten-free if made in the U.S. or Canada.

Green Lights: (no gluten)

almond flour	corn, cornmeal	meat and poultry	sorghum flour
baking soda	corn grits	millet	soy, soy flour
beans	corn tortillas	mono and diglycerides	sweet rice flour (glutinous rice flour)
buckwheat	dairy	nuts	tapioca
carob	distilled alcohol	oils and fats	tofu
carrageenan	eggs	polenta	vegetables (fresh, canned, or frozen without sauce/ seasonings)
cellophane noodles (bean thread noodles)	fruit, fresh, frozen, or dried	potatoes	
	guar gum	quinoa	vinegar (except malt)
cheese	lentils	rice, rice flour	xanthan gum
chickpea flour (garbanzo flour, besan flour)	maltodextrin	rice noodles	
	masa harina	seafood	

Slow Cooking Hints and Tips

To get the most from your **CROCK-POT®** slow cooker, keep the following hints and tips in mind.

Adding Ingredients at the End of the Cooking Time

Certain ingredients are best added toward the end of the cooking time. These include:
- **Milk, sour cream, and yogurt:** Add during the last 15 minutes.
- **Seafood and fish:** Add during the last 15 to 30 minutes.
- **Fresh herbs:** Fresh herbs such as basil will darken with long cooking, so if you want colorful fresh herbs, add them during the last 15 minutes of cooking or directly to the dish just before serving it.

Pasta and Rice

Converted rice holds up best through slow cooking. If the rice doesn't seem completely cooked after the suggested time, add an extra ½ cup to 1 cup of liquid per cup of rice, and extend the cooking time by 30 to 60 minutes.

Cooking Temperatures and Food Safety

According to the U.S. Department of Agriculture, bacteria in food is killed at a temperature of 165°F. As a result, it's important to follow the recommended cooking times and to keep the cover on your **CROCK-POT®** slow cooker during the cooking process to maintain food-safe temperatures. Slow-cooked meats and poultry are best when simmered gently for the period of time that allows the connective tissues to break down, yielding meat that is fall-off-the-bone tender and juicy.

Browning Meat

Meat will not brown as it would if it were cooked in a skillet or oven at a high temperature. It's not necessary to brown meat before slow cooking. However, if you prefer the look and flavor of browned meat, just brown it in a large skillet coated with oil, butter, or nonstick cooking spray, then place the browned ingredients into the stoneware and follow the recipe as written.

Herbs and Spices

When cooking with your **CROCK-POT®** slow cooker, use dried and ground herbs and spices, which work well during long cook times. However, the flavor and aroma of crushed or ground herbs may differ depending on their shelf life, and their flavor can lessen during the extended cooking time in the **CROCK-POT®** slow cooker.

Cooking for Larger Quantity Yields

Follow these guidelines to make a bigger batch in a larger unit, such as a 5-, 6- or 7-quart **CROCK-POT®** slow cooker:
- Roasted meats, chicken, and turkey quantities may be doubled or tripled, and seasonings adjusted by half. Caution: Flavorful dried spices such as garlic or chili powder will intensify during long, slow cooking. Add just 25 to 50 percent more spices, as needed, to balance the flavors.

• When preparing a soup or a stew, you may double all ingredients except the liquids, seasonings, and dried herbs. Increase liquid volume by half, or adjust as needed.

• To avoid over or undercooking, always fill the stoneware ½ to ¾ full and conform to the recommended cook times (unless instructed otherwise by our **CROCK-POT**® slow cooker recipes).

• Do not double thickeners, such as cornstarch, at the beginning. You may always add more thickener later if it's necessary.

Cooking with Frozen Foods

Slow cooking frozen foods requires a longer cook time than fresh foods because the food needs more time to come up to safe internal temperatures. Meats also will require additional time to allow them to become tender. If there is any question about the cooking time, use

a thermometer to ensure meats are cooking appropriately.

Removable Stoneware

The removable stoneware in your **CROCK-POT**® slow cooker makes cleaning easy. However, the stoneware insert can be damaged by sudden changes in temperature. Here are tips on the use and care of your stoneware:

• Don't preheat the **CROCK-POT**® slow cooker. Don't place a cold insert into a preheated base.

• Don't place a hot insert on a cold surface or in the refrigerator; don't fill it with cold water.

• Never place stoneware in the freezer.

• Don't use the stoneware insert if it's cracked; replace it.

• For further safety tips, please refer to the instruction manual that came with your **CROCK-POT**® slow cooker.

Minestrone alla Milanese

- 2 cans (about 14 ounces *each*) gluten-free beef broth
- 1 can (about 14 ounces) diced tomatoes
- 1 cup diced red potatoes
- 1 cup chopped carrots
- 1 cup chopped green cabbage
- 1 cup sliced zucchini
- ¾ cup chopped onion
- ¾ cup chopped celery
- ¾ cup sliced fresh green beans
- ¾ cup water
- 2 tablespoons olive oil
- 1 clove garlic, minced
- ½ teaspoon dried basil
- ¼ teaspoon dried rosemary
- 1 whole bay leaf
- 1 can (about 15 ounces) cannellini beans, rinsed and drained
- Grated Parmesan cheese (optional)

1. Combine broth, tomatoes, potatoes, carrots, cabbage, zucchini, onion, celery, green beans, water, oil, garlic, basil, rosemary and bay leaf in **CROCK-POT®** slow cooker; mix well. Cover; cook on LOW 5 to 6 hours.

2. Add cannellini beans. Cover; cook on LOW 1 hour or until vegetables are tender. Remove and discard bay leaf. Top with cheese, if desired.

Makes 8 to 10 servings

Hearty Lentil and Root Vegetable Stew

2 cans (about 14 ounces *each*) gluten-free chicken broth

1½ cups turnips, cut into 1-inch cubes

1 cup dried red lentils, rinsed and sorted

1 medium onion, cut into ½-inch wedges

2 medium carrots, cut into 1-inch pieces

1 medium red bell pepper, cut into 1-inch pieces

½ teaspoon dried oregano

⅛ teaspoon red pepper flakes

1 tablespoon olive oil

½ teaspoon salt

4 slices bacon, crisp-cooked and crumbled

½ cup finely chopped green onions

1. Combine broth, turnips, lentils, onion, carrots, bell pepper, oregano and red pepper flakes in **CROCK-POT®** slow cooker; mix well. Cover; cook on LOW 6 hours or on HIGH 3 hours.

2. Stir in oil and salt. Top each serving with bacon and green onions.

Makes 8 servings

Northwest Beef and Vegetable Soup

2 tablespoons olive oil

1 pound cubed beef stew meat

1 onion, chopped

1 clove garlic, minced

8 cups water

3½ cups canned crushed tomatoes, undrained

1 butternut squash, peeled and diced

1 can (about 15 ounces) white beans, rinsed and drained

1 turnip, peeled and diced

1 large potato, diced

2 stalks celery, sliced

2 tablespoons minced fresh basil

1½ teaspoons salt

1 teaspoon black pepper

1. Heat oil in large skillet over medium heat. Brown beef 6 to 8 minutes on all sides. Add onion and garlic during last few minutes of browning. Transfer to **CROCK-POT®** slow cooker.

2. Add water, tomatoes, squash, beans, turnip, potato, celery, basil, salt and pepper; stir to combine. Cover; cook on HIGH 2 hours.

3. Turn **CROCK-POT®** slow cooker to LOW. Cover; cook on LOW 4 to 6 hours, stirring occasionally.

Makes 6 to 8 servings

Roasted Tomato-Basil Soup

2 cans (28 ounces *each*) whole tomatoes, drained, 3 cups liquid reserved

2½ tablespoons packed dark brown sugar

1 medium onion, finely chopped

3 cups gluten-free vegetable broth

3 tablespoons tomato paste

¼ teaspoon ground allspice

1 can (5 ounces) evaporated milk

¼ cup shredded fresh basil (about 10 large leaves)

Salt and black pepper

1. Preheat oven to 450°F. Line baking sheet with foil; spray with nonstick cooking spray. Arrange tomatoes on foil in single layer. Sprinkle with brown sugar; top with onion. Bake 25 minutes or until tomatoes look dry and light brown. Let tomatoes cool slightly; finely chop.

2. Place tomato mixture, 3 cups reserved liquid from tomatoes, broth, tomato paste and allspice in **CROCK-POT®** slow cooker; mix well. Cover; cook on LOW 8 hours or on HIGH 4 hours.

3. Add evaporated milk and basil; season with salt and pepper. Cover; cook on HIGH 30 minutes or until heated through.

Makes 6 servings

Creamy Cauliflower Bisque

1 pound frozen cauliflower florets

1 pound baking potatoes, cut into 1-inch cubes

1 cup chopped yellow onion

2 cans (about 14 ounces *each*) gluten-free vegetable broth

½ teaspoon dried thyme

¼ teaspoon garlic powder

⅛ teaspoon ground red pepper

1 cup evaporated milk

2 tablespoons butter

½ teaspoon salt

¼ teaspoon black pepper

1 cup (4 ounces) shredded sharp Cheddar cheese

¼ cup finely chopped fresh Italian parsley

¼ cup finely chopped green onions

1. Combine cauliflower, potatoes, onion, broth, thyme, garlic powder and ground red pepper in **CROCK-POT®** slow cooker. Cover; cook on LOW 8 hours or on HIGH 4 hours.

2. Pour soup into blender or food processor in batches; blend until smooth. Return puréed batches to **CROCK-POT®** slow cooker. Add evaporated milk, butter, salt and black pepper; stir until blended. Top individual servings with cheese, parsley and green onions.

Makes 9 servings

New Mexican Green Chile Pork Stew

1½ pounds boneless pork shoulder, cut into 1-inch cubes

2 medium baking potatoes or sweet potatoes, cut into 1-inch pieces

1 cup chopped onion

1 cup frozen corn, thawed

1 can (4 ounces) diced mild green chiles

1 jar (16 ounces) salsa verde (green salsa)

2 teaspoons sugar

2 teaspoons ground cumin or chili powder

1 teaspoon dried oregano

Hot cooked rice

¼ cup chopped fresh cilantro (optional)

1. Place pork, potatoes, onion, corn and chiles in **CROCK-POT®** slow cooker.

2. Stir salsa, sugar, cumin and oregano in medium bowl until blended. Pour over pork and vegetables. Cover; cook on LOW 6 to 8 hours or on HIGH 4 to 5 hours. Serve stew over rice. Garnish with cilantro.

Makes 6 servings

Tip: Root vegetables such as potatoes can sometimes take longer to cook in a **CROCK-POT®** slow cooker than meat. Place uniformly cut vegetables along the sides or on the bottom of the **CROCK-POT®** slow cooker when possible.

Asian Beef Stew

2 onions, cut into ¼-inch slices

1½ pounds boneless beef round steak, sliced thin across the grain

2 stalks celery, sliced

2 carrots, sliced

1 cup sliced mushrooms

1 cup orange juice

1 cup gluten-free beef broth

⅓ cup gluten-free hoisin sauce

2 tablespoons cornstarch

1 to 2 teaspoons Chinese five-spice powder or curry powder

1 cup frozen peas, thawed

Hot cooked rice

Chopped fresh cilantro (optional)

1. Layer onions, beef, celery, carrots and mushrooms in **CROCK-POT®** slow cooker.

2. Combine orange juice, broth, hoisin sauce, cornstarch and five-spice powder in small bowl. Pour into **CROCK-POT®** slow cooker. Cover; cook on HIGH 5 hours.

3. Stir in peas. Cover; cook on HIGH 20 minutes or until peas are tender. Serve over rice. Garnish with cilantro.

Makes 6 servings

Mexican Cheese Soup

1 **pound ground beef**

1 **pound pasteurized process cheese product, cubed**

1 **can (about 15 ounces) kidney beans, rinsed and drained**

1 **can (about 14 ounces) diced tomatoes with mild green chiles**

1 **can (about 14 ounces) stewed tomatoes, undrained**

1 **can (8¾ ounces) corn, undrained**

1 **envelope taco seasoning mix**

1 **jalapeño pepper, seeded and diced* (optional)**

Corn chips (optional)

*Jalapeño peppers can sting and irritate the skin, so wear rubber gloves when handling peppers and do not touch your eyes.

1. Coat inside of **CROCK-POT®** slow cooker with nonstick cooking spray. Brown beef 6 to 8 minutes in large skillet over medium-high heat, stirring to break up meat. Drain fat.

2. Add beef, cheese product, beans, tomatoes with chiles, stewed tomatoes, corn, taco seasoning mix and jalapeño pepper, if desired, to **CROCK-POT®** slow cooker; mix well. Cover; cook on LOW 4 to 5 hours or on HIGH 3 hours. Serve with corn chips, if desired.

Makes 6 to 8 servings

Gluten-Free Tip: Most spice mixes are gluten-free, but it's still a good idea to check the ingredients label to make sure there are no hidden problems. Fortunately with labeling laws, suspect ingredients now have to list wheat if they are made from it.

Caribbean Sweet Potato and Bean Stew

2 sweet potatoes (about 1 pound), cut into 1-inch cubes

2 cups frozen cut green beans

1 can (about 15 ounces) black beans, rinsed and drained

1 can (about 14 ounces) gluten-free vegetable broth

1 onion, sliced

2 teaspoons Caribbean jerk seasoning

½ teaspoon dried thyme

¼ teaspoon salt

¼ teaspoon ground cinnamon

⅓ cup slivered almonds, toasted*

To toast almonds, spread in single layer in heavy skillet. Cook and stir over medium heat 1 to 2 minutes or until nuts are lightly browned.

Combine sweet potatoes, green beans, black beans, broth, onion, Caribbean jerk seasoning, thyme, salt and cinnamon in **CROCK-POT®** slow cooker. Cover; cook on LOW 5 to 6 hours or until vegetables are tender. Sprinkle with almonds.

Makes 4 servings

Easy Corn Chowder

2 cans (about 14 ounces *each*) gluten-free chicken broth

1 bag (16 ounces) frozen corn, thawed

3 small red potatoes, cut into ½-inch pieces

1 red bell pepper, diced

1 medium onion, diced

1 stalk celery, sliced

½ teaspoon salt

½ teaspoon black pepper

¼ teaspoon ground coriander

½ cup heavy cream

8 slices bacon, crisp-cooked and crumbled

1. Place broth, corn, potatoes, bell pepper, onion, celery, salt, black pepper and coriander in **CROCK-POT®** slow cooker. Cover; cook on LOW 7 to 8 hours.

2. Partially mash soup mixture with potato masher to thicken. Turn **CROCK-POT®** slow cooker to HIGH. Stir in cream; cook, uncovered, on HIGH 30 minutes or until heated through. Sprinkle with bacon.

Makes 6 servings

Note: Defrost vegetables before cooking them in the **CROCK-POT®** slow cooker.

Irish Stew

1 cup gluten-free chicken broth

1 teaspoon dried marjoram

1 teaspoon dried parsley

¾ teaspoon salt

½ teaspoon garlic powder

¼ teaspoon black pepper

1¼ pounds white potatoes, cut into 1-inch pieces

1 pound cubed lamb stew meat

8 ounces frozen cut green beans, thawed

2 small leeks, cut lengthwise into halves, then crosswise into slices

1½ cups sliced carrots

1. Combine broth, marjoram, parsley, salt, garlic powder and pepper in **CROCK-POT®** slow cooker; mix well.

2. Layer potatoes, lamb, green beans, leeks and carrots in **CROCK-POT®** slow cooker. Cover; cook on LOW 7 to 9 hours.

Makes 6 servings

Tip: For a thicker stew, stir ¼ cup water into 1 tablespoon cornstarch in small bowl until smooth. Whisk into cooking liquid in **CROCK-POT®** slow cooker; cook on HIGH 10 to 15 minutes or until thickened.

Chicken and Sweet Potato Stew

4 boneless, skinless chicken breasts, cut into bite-size pieces

2 medium sweet potatoes, cubed

2 medium Yukon Gold potatoes, cubed

2 medium carrots, cut into ½-inch slices

1 can (28 ounces) whole stewed tomatoes

1 cup gluten-free chicken broth

1 teaspoon salt

1 teaspoon paprika

1 teaspoon celery seed

½ teaspoon black pepper

⅛ teaspoon ground cinnamon

⅛ teaspoon ground nutmeg

¼ cup fresh basil, chopped

Combine chicken, potatoes, carrots, tomatoes, broth, salt, paprika, celery seed, pepper, cinnamon and nutmeg in **CROCK-POT®** slow cooker. Cover; cook on LOW 6 to 8 hours or on HIGH 3 to 4 hours. Sprinkle each serving with basil.

Makes 6 servings

Beef Stew with Bacon, Onion and Sweet Potatoes

1 pound cubed beef stew meat	2 slices thick-cut bacon, chopped
1 can (about 14 ounces) gluten-free beef broth	1 teaspoon dried thyme
2 medium sweet potatoes, cut into 2-inch pieces	1 teaspoon salt
	¼ teaspoon black pepper
1 large onion, chopped	2 tablespoons water
	2 tablespoons cornstarch

1. Coat inside of **CROCK-POT®** slow cooker with nonstick cooking spray. Combine beef, broth, sweet potatoes, onion, bacon, thyme, salt and pepper in **CROCK-POT®** slow cooker; mix well.

2. Cover; cook on LOW 7 to 8 hours or on HIGH 4 to 5 hours. Remove beef and vegetables to serving bowl using slotted spoon. Cover and keep warm.

3. Stir water into cornstarch in small bowl until smooth. Whisk into cooking liquid in **CROCK-POT®** slow cooker. Cover; cook on LOW 15 minutes or until thickened. Serve sauce over beef and vegetables.

Makes 4 servings

Chicken Fiesta Soup

4 boneless, skinless chicken breasts, cooked and shredded

1 can (about 14 ounces) stewed tomatoes, drained

2 cans (4 ounces *each*) chopped mild green chiles

1 can (28 ounces) gluten-free enchilada sauce

1 can (about 14 ounces) gluten-free chicken broth

1 cup finely chopped onion

2 cloves garlic, minced

1 teaspoon ground cumin

1 teaspoon chili powder

1 teaspoon salt

¾ teaspoon black pepper

¼ cup finely chopped fresh cilantro

1 cup frozen corn, thawed

1 yellow squash, diced

1 zucchini, diced

8 corn tostada shells, crumbled

2 cups (8 ounces) shredded Cheddar cheese

Combine chicken, tomatoes, chiles, enchilada sauce, broth, onion, garlic, cumin, chili powder, salt, pepper, cilantro, corn, squash and zucchini in **CROCK-POT®** slow cooker. Cover; cook on LOW 8 hours. Ladle soup into bowls. Garnish with tostada shells and cheese.

Makes 8 servings

Hearty Lentil Stew

1 cup dried lentils, rinsed and sorted

1 package (16 ounces) frozen cut green beans, thawed

2 cups cauliflower florets

1 cup onion, chopped

1 cup baby carrots, cut in half crosswise

3 cups gluten-free chicken broth

2 teaspoons ground cumin

¾ teaspoon ground ginger

1 can (about 15 ounces) chunky tomato sauce with garlic and herbs

½ cup dry-roasted peanuts, chopped

1. Place lentils in **CROCK-POT®** slow cooker. Top with green beans, cauliflower, onion and carrots.

2. Combine broth, cumin and ginger in large bowl; mix well. Pour over vegetables in **CROCK-POT®** slow cooker. Cover; cook on LOW 9 to 11 hours.

3. Stir in tomato sauce. Cover; cook on LOW 10 minutes. Ladle stew into bowls. Sprinkle with peanuts.

Makes 6 servings

Chicken Soup

6 cups gluten-free chicken broth

1½ pounds boneless, skinless chicken breasts, cubed

2 cups sliced carrots

1 cup sliced mushrooms

1 red bell pepper, chopped

1 onion, chopped

2 tablespoons grated fresh ginger

3 teaspoons minced garlic

½ teaspoon red pepper flakes

Salt and black pepper

Place broth, chicken, carrots, mushrooms, bell pepper, onion, ginger, garlic, red pepper flakes, salt and black pepper in **CROCK-POT**® slow cooker. Cover; cook on LOW 6 to 7 hours or on HIGH 3 to 3½ hours.

Makes 4 to 6 servings

Tip: Skinless chicken is best for the **CROCK-POT**® slow cooker, because the skin tends to shrivel and curl during cooking.

Sweet Potato Stew

1 cup chopped onion

1 cup chopped celery

1 cup grated sweet potato

1 cup gluten-free vegetable broth or water

2 slices bacon, crisp-cooked and crumbled

1 cup half-and-half

Black pepper

¼ cup minced fresh Italian parsley (optional)

1. Place onion, celery, sweet potato, broth and bacon in **CROCK-POT®** slow cooker. Cover; cook on LOW 6 hours.

2. Turn **CROCK-POT®** slow cooker to HIGH. Add enough half-and-half to **CROCK-POT®** slow cooker to reach desired consistency. Cook, uncovered, on HIGH 30 minutes or until heated through. Season with pepper. Garnish with parsley.

Makes 4 servings

Chicken and Chile Pepper Stew

1 pound boneless, skinless chicken thighs, cut into ½-inch pieces

1 pound small potatoes, unpeeled and cut lengthwise into halves, then crosswise into slices

1 cup chopped onion

2 poblano peppers, seeded and cut into ½-inch pieces*

1 jalapeño pepper, seeded and finely chopped*

3 cloves garlic, minced

3 cups gluten-free chicken broth

1 can (about 14 ounces) diced tomatoes

2 tablespoons chili powder

1 teaspoon dried oregano

Corn tortilla chips (optional)

*Poblano and jalapeño peppers can sting and irritate the skin, so wear rubber gloves when handling peppers and do not touch your eyes.

1. Place chicken, potatoes, onion, poblano peppers, jalapeño pepper and garlic in **CROCK-POT®** slow cooker.

2. Stir broth, tomatoes, chili powder and oregano in large bowl until well blended. Pour into **CROCK-POT®** slow cooker. Cover; cook on LOW 8 to 9 hours. Serve with tortilla chips, if desired.

Makes 6 servings

Seafood Stew

1 can (28 ounces) fire-roasted tomatoes

1 can (about 15 ounces) tomato sauce

1 pound frozen calamari rings, thawed

1 package (8 ounces) yellow rice

2 cans (about 6 ounces *each*) clams, liquid drained and reserved

4 cloves garlic, minced

2 tablespoons fennel seeds

1 pound medium raw shrimp, peeled, deveined and cut in half (with tails on)

1 teaspoon grated lemon peel

½ teaspoon black pepper

1. Stir tomatoes, tomato sauce, calamari, rice, reserved clam juice, garlic and fennel seeds into **CROCK-POT®** slow cooker. Cover; cook on LOW 5 to 6 hours or on HIGH 2½ to 3 hours or until calamari are tender.

2. Stir clams, shrimp, lemon peel and pepper into **CROCK-POT®** slow cooker. Cover; cook on HIGH 5 minutes or until shrimp are pink and opaque.

Makes 6 servings

Panama Pork Stew

2 small sweet potatoes (about ¾ pound), cut into 2-inch pieces	1¼ pounds cubed pork stew meat
1 package (10 ounces) frozen corn, thawed	1 can (about 14 ounces) diced tomatoes
1 package (9 ounces) frozen cut green beans, thawed	¼ cup water
1 cup chopped onion	1 to 2 tablespoons chili powder
	½ teaspoon salt
	½ teaspoon ground coriander

1. Place potatoes, corn, green beans and onion in **CROCK-POT®** slow cooker. Top with pork.

2. Combine tomatoes, water, chili powder, salt and coriander in medium bowl. Pour over pork in **CROCK-POT®** slow cooker. Cover; cook on LOW 7 to 9 hours.

Makes 6 servings

Thai Chicken

2½ **pounds chicken pieces**	1 **teaspoon minced fresh ginger**
1 **cup hot salsa**	**Hot cooked rice**
¼ **cup peanut butter**	½ **cup peanuts, chopped**
2 **tablespoons lime juice**	2 **tablespoons chopped fresh**
1 **tablespoon gluten-free soy sauce**	**cilantro**

1. Place chicken in **CROCK-POT®** slow cooker. Combine salsa, peanut butter, lime juice, soy sauce and ginger in small bowl; stir until blended. Pour over chicken.

2. Cover; cook on LOW 8 to 9 hours or on HIGH 3 to 4 hours. Serve over rice. Top with sauce, peanuts and cilantro.

Makes 6 servings

Spanish Chicken with Rice

2 tablespoons olive oil

11 ounces gluten-free cooked kielbasa or linguiça sausage, sliced into ½-inch rounds

6 boneless, skinless chicken thighs (about 1 pound)

1 onion, chopped

5 cloves garlic, minced

2 cups converted long grain rice

½ cup diced carrots

1 red bell pepper, chopped

½ teaspoon salt

¼ teaspoon black pepper

¼ teaspoon saffron threads (optional)

3½ cups warm gluten-free chicken broth

½ cup peas

1. Heat oil in medium skillet over medium heat. Add sausage; cook and stir 6 to 8 minutes or until browned. Transfer to **CROCK-POT®** slow cooker using slotted spoon.

2. Brown chicken 5 to 7 minutes on all sides in same skillet. Transfer to **CROCK-POT®** slow cooker. Add onion to skillet; cook and stir 5 minutes or until soft. Stir in garlic; cook 30 seconds. Transfer to **CROCK-POT®** slow cooker.

3. Add rice, carrots, bell pepper, salt, black pepper and saffron, if desired, to **CROCK-POT®** slow cooker. Pour in broth. Cover; cook on HIGH 3½ to 4 hours.

4. Stir in peas. Cover; cook on HIGH 15 minutes or until heated through.

Makes 6 servings

Serving Suggestion: Serve with gluten-free jalapeño cornbread, if desired.

Basque Chicken with Peppers

1 whole chicken (4 pounds), cut into 8 pieces	8 ounces small brown mushrooms, halved
2 teaspoons salt, divided	1 can (about 14 ounces) stewed tomatoes, undrained
1 teaspoon black pepper, divided	½ cup gluten-free chicken broth
1½ tablespoons olive oil	½ cup Rioja wine
1 onion, chopped	3 ounces tomato paste
1 medium green bell pepper, cut into strips	2 cloves garlic, minced
1 medium yellow bell pepper, cut into strips	1 sprig fresh marjoram
	1 teaspoon smoked paprika
1 medium red bell pepper, cut into strips	Hot cooked rice
	4 ounces chopped prosciutto

1. Season chicken with 1 teaspoon salt and ½ teaspoon black pepper. Heat oil in large skillet over medium-high heat. Add chicken in batches; cook 5 to 7 minutes on each side or until browned. Transfer each batch to **CROCK-POT®** slow cooker.

2. Reduce heat to medium-low. Stir in onion; cook and stir 3 minutes or until softened. Add bell peppers and mushrooms; cook 3 minutes. Add tomatoes, broth, wine, tomato paste, garlic, marjoram, remaining 1 teaspoon salt, paprika and remaining ½ teaspoon black pepper to skillet; simmer 3 to 4 minutes. Pour over chicken in **CROCK-POT®** slow cooker. Cover; cook on LOW 5 to 6 hours or on HIGH 4 hours. Serve chicken over rice; top with vegetables and sauce. Sprinkle with prosciutto.

Makes 4 to 6 servings

Indian-Style Curried Drumsticks

12 chicken drumsticks (about 3 pounds)

1 cinnamon stick

2 tablespoons vegetable oil

1 large onion, diced

3 tablespoons tomato paste

1 tablespoon ground cumin

1 tablespoon grated fresh ginger

1 tablespoon minced garlic

2 teaspoons salt

2 teaspoons ground turmeric

1 teaspoon ground coriander

½ teaspoon black pepper

8 medium red potatoes, cut in half (about 1¾ pounds total)

1¼ cups gluten-free chicken broth

1 cup frozen peas, thawed

1. Place drumsticks and cinnamon stick in **CROCK-POT**® slow cooker. Heat oil in medium saucepan over medium heat. Add onion; cook and stir until softened. Add tomato paste, cumin, ginger, garlic, salt, turmeric, coriander and pepper; cook and stir 2 minutes. Add onion mixture, potatoes and broth to **CROCK-POT**® slow cooker. Cover; cook on LOW 6 hours.

2. Remove chicken and potatoes from **CROCK-POT**® slow cooker using slotted spoon. Stir in peas. Cover; cook on LOW 5 minutes or until peas are heated through. Serve drumsticks and potatoes topped with curry.

Makes 4 to 6 servings

Jamaica-Me-Crazy Chicken Tropicale

2 sweet potatoes, cut into 2-inch pieces

1 can (20 ounces) pineapple tidbits in pineapple juice, drained and juice reserved

1 can (8 ounces) water chestnuts, drained and sliced

1 cup golden raisins

4 boneless, skinless chicken breasts

4 teaspoons Caribbean jerk seasoning

¼ cup dried onion flakes

3 tablespoons grated fresh ginger

2 tablespoons gluten-free Worcestershire sauce

1 tablespoon grated lime peel

1 teaspoon whole cumin seeds, slightly crushed

Hot cooked rice (optional)

1. Place sweet potatoes in **CROCK-POT®** slow cooker. Add pineapple tidbits, water chestnuts and raisins; mix well.

2. Sprinkle chicken with Caribbean jerk seasoning. Place chicken on top of sweet potato mixture.

3. Combine reserved pineapple juice, onion flakes, ginger, Worcestershire sauce, lime peel and cumin seeds in small bowl; stir until blended. Pour over chicken. Cover; cook on LOW 7 to 9 hours or on HIGH 3 to 4 hours. Serve with rice, if desired.

Makes 4 servings

Herbed Artichoke Chicken

1½ pounds boneless, skinless chicken breasts

1 can (about 14 ounces) whole tomatoes, drained and chopped

1 can (14 ounces) artichoke hearts in water, drained

1 cup gluten-free chicken broth

1 small onion, chopped

½ cup kalamata olives, pitted and sliced

¼ cup dry white wine

3 tablespoons quick-cooking tapioca

2 teaspoons curry powder

1 tablespoon chopped fresh Italian parsley

1 teaspoon dried sweet basil

1 teaspoon dried thyme

½ teaspoon salt

½ teaspoon black pepper

Combine chicken, tomatoes, artichokes, broth, onion, olives, wine, tapioca, curry powder, parsley, basil, thyme, salt and pepper in **CROCK-POT®** slow cooker; mix well. Cover; cook on LOW 6 to 8 hours or on HIGH 3½ to 4 hours.

Makes 6 servings

Tip: For a 5-, 6- or 7-quart **CROCK-POT®** slow cooker, double all ingredients, except for the chicken broth and white wine. Increase the chicken broth and white wine by one half.

Easy Cheesy Aruban-Inspired Chicken

1 can (about 14 ounces) diced tomatoes

½ cup gluten-free chicken broth

¼ cup ketchup

3 cloves garlic, crushed

2 teaspoons yellow mustard

1 teaspoon gluten-free Worcestershire sauce

¾ teaspoon hot pepper sauce

½ teaspoon salt

¼ teaspoon black pepper

1 large onion, thinly sliced

1 large green bell pepper, thinly sliced

¼ cup sliced black olives

¼ cup raisins

1 tablespoon capers

4 to 6 boneless, skinless chicken thighs or breasts

1½ cups (6 ounces) shredded Edam or Gouda cheese

Hot cooked rice

2 tablespoons chopped fresh Italian parsley

1. Coat inside of **CROCK-POT**® slow cooker with nonstick cooking spray. Add tomatoes, broth, ketchup, garlic, mustard, Worcestershire sauce, hot pepper sauce, salt and black pepper; stir until well blended.

2. Add onion, bell pepper, olives, raisins and capers; stir until well blended. Add chicken; stir to coat with sauce mixture. Cover; cook on HIGH 3 to 4 hours.

3. Turn off heat. Sprinkle cheese over chicken. Cover; let stand 3 to 5 minutes or until cheese is melted. Serve over rice. Sprinkle with parsley.

Makes 4 servings

Chicken Teriyaki

1 **pound boneless, skinless chicken tenders**

1 **can (6 ounces) pineapple juice**

¼ **cup gluten-free soy sauce**

1 **tablespoon sugar**

1 **tablespoon minced fresh ginger**

1 **tablespoon minced garlic**

1 **tablespoon vegetable oil**

1 **tablespoon molasses**

24 **cherry tomatoes (optional)**

2 **cups hot cooked rice**

Combine chicken, pineapple juice, soy sauce, sugar, ginger, garlic, oil, molasses and tomatoes, if desired, in **CROCK-POT®** slow cooker. Cover; cook on LOW 2 hours. Serve chicken and sauce over rice.

Makes 4 servings

Gluten-Free Tip: Rice can be a staple in a gluten-free diet. There are many varieties that are usually classified by the size of the grain—short, medium or long. Long grain rice cooks up fluffy and dry, so it's good to serve under a saucy main course like this Chicken Teriyaki.

Forty-Clove Chicken

1 cut-up whole chicken (about 3 pounds)
Salt and black pepper
1 to 2 tablespoons olive oil
¼ cup dry white wine
2 tablespoons chopped fresh Italian parsley *or* 2 teaspoons dried parsley

2 tablespoons dry vermouth
2 teaspoons dried basil
1 teaspoon dried oregano
Pinch red pepper flakes
40 cloves garlic (about 2 heads)
4 stalks celery, sliced
Juice and peel of 1 lemon
Sprigs fresh thyme (optional)

1. Season chicken with salt and black pepper. Heat oil in large skillet over medium heat. Add chicken to skillet; cook 5 to 7 minutes on each side or until browned. Remove to platter.

2. Combine wine, parsley, vermouth, basil, oregano and red pepper flakes in large bowl. Add garlic and celery; coat well. Transfer garlic and celery to **CROCK-POT®** slow cooker using slotted spoon. Add chicken to remaining herb mixture; coat well. Place chicken on top of garlic mixture in **CROCK-POT®** slow cooker.

3. Sprinkle lemon juice and peel over chicken. Cover; cook on LOW 6 hours. Garnish with thyme.

Makes 4 to 6 servings

Chicken and Wild Rice Casserole

- 3 tablespoons olive oil
- 2 slices bacon, crisp-cooked and chopped
- 1½ pounds chicken thighs, trimmed
- ½ cup diced onion
- ½ cup diced celery
- 2 tablespoons gluten-free Worcestershire sauce
- ¾ teaspoon salt
- ½ teaspoon dried sage
- ¼ teaspoon black pepper

- 1 cup converted long grain white rice
- 1 package (4 ounces) wild rice
- 6 ounces brown mushrooms, wiped clean and quartered*
- 3 cups warm gluten-free chicken broth**
- 2 tablespoons chopped fresh Italian parsley (optional)

*Use "baby bellas" or cremini mushrooms. Or you may substitute white button mushrooms.

**Use enough broth to cover chicken.

1. Coat bottom of **CROCK-POT**® slow cooker with oil. Place bacon and chicken, skin side down in **CROCK-POT**® slow cooker. Layer with onion, celery, Worcestershire sauce, salt, sage, pepper, white rice, wild rice, mushrooms and broth. Cover; cook on LOW 3 to 4 hours.

2. Turn off heat. Uncover; let stand 15 minutes before serving. Remove chicken skin, if desired. Garnish with parsley.

Makes 4 to 6 servings

Dijon Chicken Thighs with Artichoke Sauce

½ cup Dijon mustard

2 tablespoons chopped garlic

½ teaspoon dried tarragon

2½ pounds skinless chicken thighs (about 8)

1 cup chopped onion

1 cup sliced mushrooms

1 jar (12 ounces) quartered marinated artichoke hearts, undrained

¼ cup chopped fresh Italian parsley

1. Combine mustard, garlic and tarragon in large bowl. Add chicken thighs; toss to coat. Transfer to **CROCK-POT®** slow cooker.

2. Add onion, mushrooms and artichokes with liquid. Cover; cook on LOW 6 to 8 hours or on HIGH 4 hours. Stir in parsley just before serving.

Makes 8 servings

Note: To skin chicken easily, grasp skin with paper towel and pull away. Repeat with fresh paper towel for each piece of chicken, discarding skins and towels.

Chicken and Spicy Black Bean Tacos

1 can (about 15 ounces) black beans, rinsed and drained

1 can (10 ounces) diced tomatoes with mild green chiles, drained

1 tablespoon plus 1 teaspoon extra virgin olive oil, divided

1½ teaspoons chili powder

¾ teaspoon ground cumin

12 ounces boneless, skinless chicken breasts

12 hard corn taco shells

Optional toppings: shredded lettuce, diced tomatoes, shredded cheese, hot pepper sauce, lime wedges and/or sliced black olives

Hot cooked rice (optional)

1. Coat inside of **CROCK-POT®** slow cooker with nonstick cooking spray. Add beans and tomatoes with chiles. Combine 1 teaspoon oil, chili powder and cumin in small bowl; rub onto chicken. Place chicken in **CROCK-POT®** slow cooker. Cover; cook on HIGH 1¾ hours.

2. Remove chicken and slice. Transfer bean mixture to bowl using slotted spoon. Stir in remaining 1 tablespoon oil.

3. To serve, warm taco shells according to package directions. Fill with equal amounts of bean mixture and chicken. Top as desired. Serve with rice, if desired.

Makes 4 servings

Curry Chicken with Peaches and Raisins

2 peaches, peeled and sliced into ¼-inch slices, reserving 8 slices for garnish
Lemon juice

4 boneless, skinless chicken thighs *or* 2 boneless, skinless chicken breasts
Salt and black pepper

1 tablespoon olive oil

⅓ cup raisins or currants, chopped

1 shallot, thinly sliced

¼ cup gluten-free chicken broth

1 tablespoon grated fresh ginger

1 tablespoon cider vinegar

2 cloves garlic, crushed

1 teaspoon ground cumin

½ teaspoon curry powder

½ teaspoon whole cloves

¼ teaspoon ground red pepper (optional)

1 teaspoon cornstarch (optional)
Hot cooked rice
Fresh cilantro leaves (optional)

1. Toss reserved slices of peaches with lemon juice in medium bowl until well coated; refrigerate. Season chicken with salt and black pepper.

2. Heat oil in large skillet over medium-high heat. Add chicken; cook 3 minutes per side or until lightly browned. Transfer to **CROCK-POT®** slow cooker. Top with remaining peaches, raisins and shallot.

3. Whisk broth, ginger, vinegar, garlic, cumin, curry powder, cloves and ground red pepper, if desired, in small bowl. Pour over chicken. Cover; cook on LOW 5 hours or on HIGH 3 to 3½ hours.

4. Transfer chicken to serving dish. Whisk cornstarch into sauce, if desired. Serve chicken over rice; top with peaches, raisins and sauce. Garnish with reserved peaches and cilantro.

Makes 2 servings

Simple Coq au Vin

4 **chicken leg quarters**	½ **cup dry red wine**
Salt and black pepper	½ **teaspoon dried basil**
2 **tablespoons olive oil**	½ **teaspoon dried thyme**
8 **ounces mushrooms, sliced**	½ **teaspoon dried oregano**
1 **onion, sliced**	**Hot cooked rice (optional)**

1. Season chicken with salt and pepper. Heat oil in large skillet over medium-high heat. Brown chicken 3 to 5 minutes on each side. Transfer to **CROCK-POT®** slow cooker.

2. Add mushrooms and onion to skillet; cook and stir until onions are tender. Add wine, scraping up any browned bits from skillet. Add mixture to **CROCK-POT®** slow cooker. Sprinkle with basil, thyme and oregano. Cover; cook on LOW 8 to 10 hours or on HIGH 3 to 4 hours. Serve sauce with chicken. Serve with rice, if desired.

Makes 4 servings

Tip: Always taste the finished dish before serving and adjust the seasonings.

Mediterranean Chicken Breasts and Wild Rice

1 pound boneless, skinless chicken breasts, lightly pounded

Kosher salt

Black pepper

1 cup wild rice blend

½ cup sun-dried tomatoes packed in oil, drained and chopped

½ cup capers, drained

10 cloves garlic, crushed

2 cups water

½ cup lemon juice

¼ cup extra virgin olive oil

1. Season chicken with salt and pepper. Place chicken in **CROCK-POT**® slow cooker. Add rice, tomatoes, capers and garlic; stir well.

2. Combine water, lemon juice and oil in small bowl; stir until blended. Pour over rice and chicken in **CROCK-POT**® slow cooker; stir to coat chicken. Cover; cook on LOW 8 hours.

Makes 4 servings

Creole Vegetables and Chicken

Nonstick cooking spray

2 cups chopped green bell peppers

1 can (about 14 ounces) diced tomatoes

1 cup chopped yellow onion

8 ounces frozen cut okra, thawed

1 cup gluten-free chicken broth

¾ cup sliced celery

2 teaspoons gluten-free Worcestershire sauce

1 teaspoon dried thyme

1 whole bay leaf

1 pound chicken tenders, cut into bite-size pieces

¾ teaspoon Creole seasoning

1½ teaspoons sugar

1 tablespoon extra virgin olive oil

Hot pepper sauce

¼ cup chopped fresh Italian parsley

1. Coat inside of **CROCK-POT®** slow cooker with cooking spray. Add bell peppers, tomatoes, onion, okra, broth, celery, Worcestershire sauce, thyme and bay leaf. Cover; cook on LOW 9 hours or on HIGH 4½ hours.

2. Coat medium skillet with cooking spray. Heat over medium-high heat. Add chicken; cook and stir 6 minutes or until just beginning to brown. Transfer chicken to **CROCK-POT®** slow cooker. Add Creole seasoning, sugar, oil and hot pepper sauce. Cover; cook on HIGH 15 minutes. Stir in parsley. Remove and discard bay leaf.

Makes 8 servings

Tip: For a thicker dish, stir ¼ cup water into 1 tablespoon cornstarch in small bowl until smooth. Whisk into cooking liquid in **CROCK-POT®** slow cooker; cook on HIGH 10 to 15 minutes or until thickened.

Stuffed Chicken Breasts

6 boneless, skinless chicken breasts	½ teaspoon garlic powder
3 cups chopped fresh spinach leaves	Black pepper
8 ounces feta cheese, crumbled	1 can (about 14 ounces) diced tomatoes
⅓ cup sun-dried tomatoes packed in oil, drained and chopped	½ cup oil-cured olives*
1 teaspoon dried basil, oregano or mint	Hot cooked polenta
1 teaspoon minced lemon peel	Lemon peel twists (optional)

*If using pitted olives, add to **CROCK-POT**® slow cooker in the final hour of cooking.*

1. Place 1 chicken breast between two pieces of plastic wrap. Using tenderizer mallet or back of skillet, pound until about ¼ inch thick. Repeat with remaining chicken.

2. Combine spinach, feta, sun-dried tomatoes, basil, lemon peel, garlic powder and pepper in medium bowl. Place chicken breasts, smooth sides down, on work surface. Place 2 tablespoons feta mixture on wide end of each breast. Roll up tightly.

3. Place rolled chicken, seam sides down, in **CROCK-POT**® slow cooker. Top with diced tomatoes and olives. Cover; cook on LOW 5½ to 6 hours or on HIGH 4 hours. Serve over polenta. Garnish with lemon twists.

Makes 6 servings

Spicy Grits with Chicken

- 4 cups gluten-free chicken broth
- 1 cup grits*
- 1 jalapeño pepper, seeded and finely chopped**
- ½ teaspoon salt
- ¼ teaspoon paprika
- ¼ teaspoon black pepper
- ¾ cup (3 ounces) shredded sharp Cheddar cheese
- 1½ cups chopped cooked chicken breast (about 12 ounces total)
- ½ cup half-and-half
- 2 tablespoons chopped fresh chives, plus additional for garnish

Use coarse, instant, yellow or stone-ground grits.

**Jalapeño peppers can sting and irritate the skin, so wear rubber gloves when handling peppers and do not touch your eyes.*

1. Combine broth, grits, jalapeño pepper, salt, paprika and black pepper in **CROCK-POT**® slow cooker; stir until blended. Cover; cook on LOW 4 hours.

2. Add cheese; stir until melted. Stir in chicken, half-and-half and 2 tablespoons chives. Cover; cook on LOW 15 minutes or until heated through. Garnish with additional chives.

Makes 6 servings

Chicken with Italian Sausage

10 ounces gluten-free bulk Italian sausage

6 boneless, skinless chicken thighs, trimmed

1 can (about 15 ounces) white beans, rinsed and drained

1 can (about 15 ounces) red beans, rinsed and drained

1 cup gluten-free chicken broth

1 onion, chopped

1 teaspoon black pepper

½ teaspoon salt

Chopped fresh Italian parsley (optional)

1. Brown sausage 6 to 8 minutes in large skillet over medium-high heat, stirring to break up meat. Drain fat. Transfer to **CROCK-POT®** slow cooker using slotted spoon.

2. Add chicken, beans, broth, onion, pepper and salt to **CROCK-POT®** slow cooker. Cover; cook on LOW 5 to 6 hours. Serve chicken with sausage and beans. Garnish with parsley.

Makes 6 servings

Easy Cheesy BBQ Chicken

- 6 boneless, skinless chicken breasts (about 1½ pounds)
- 1 bottle (26 ounces) gluten-free barbecue sauce
- 6 slices bacon, crisp-cooked and cut in half
- 6 slices Swiss cheese

1. Coat inside of **CROCK-POT®** slow cooker with nonstick cooking spray. Place chicken in **CROCK-POT®** slow cooker. Cover with barbecue sauce. Cover; cook on LOW 8 to 9 hours. (If sauce becomes too thick during cooking, add a small amount of water.)

2. Place 2 bacon halves and 1 cheese slice on each chicken breast in **CROCK-POT®** slow cooker. Turn **CROCK-POT®** slow cooker to HIGH. Cover; cook on HIGH 10 to 15 minutes or until cheese is melted.

Makes 6 servings

Tip: To cleanup any sticky barbecue sauce residue, soak the stoneware in hot sudsy water, then scrub it with a plastic or nylon scrubber. Don't use steel wool.

Best Asian-Style Ribs

2 full racks baby back pork ribs, split into 3 sections each

6 ounces gluten-free hoisin sauce

½ cup maraschino cherries, drained

½ cup rice wine vinegar

2 tablespoons minced fresh ginger

4 green onions, chopped (optional)

Combine ribs, hoisin sauce, cherries, vinegar and ginger in **CROCK-POT**® slow cooker. Cover; cook on LOW 6 to 7 hours or on HIGH 3 to 3½ hours. Garnish with green onions.

Makes 6 to 8 servings

Harvest Bistro Pork Pot Roast

2 large onions, peeled and quartered

3 stalks celery, cut into 1- to 2-inch pieces

1 cup fresh whole cranberries

1 large pear, cored and cut into 8 wedges

1 large red cooking apple, cored and cut into 8 wedges

1 quince, peeled and chopped (optional)

⅔ cup packed dark brown sugar

2 tablespoons fresh thyme *or* 2 teaspoons dried thyme, plus additional for garnish

2 teaspoons salt, divided

3 pounds lean pork butt roast, cut into 2- to 3-inch pieces

1 cup gluten-free chicken broth

6 to 8 ounces Brie cheese, chopped

1. Combine onions, celery, cranberries, pear, apple and quince, if desired, in **CROCK-POT®** slow cooker. Sprinkle with brown sugar, 2 tablespoons thyme and 1 teaspoon salt. Place pork on top; pour broth over pork. Sprinkle with ½ teaspoon salt. Cover; cook on LOW 7 hours.

2. Sprinkle cheese over pork. Cover; cook on LOW 1 hour. Remove pork to serving platter. Arrange vegetables and fruits around pork. Season with remaining ½ teaspoon salt. Garnish with additional thyme.

Makes 6 to 8 servings

Spicy Asian Pork Wraps

1 boneless pork sirloin roast (about 3 pounds), cut into 2 to 3 pieces

½ cup gluten-free soy sauce

1 tablespoon gluten-free chili garlic sauce

2 teaspoons minced fresh ginger

2 tablespoons water

1 tablespoon cornstarch

2 teaspoons dark sesame oil

1 cup shredded carrot

Lettuce leaves (optional)

1. Combine pork, soy sauce, chili garlic sauce and ginger in **CROCK-POT®** slow cooker; mix well. Cover; cook on LOW 8 to 10 hours.

2. Remove roast to cutting board; shred with two forks. Let cooking liquid stand 5 minutes. Skim off and discard fat.

3. Stir water, cornstarch and oil in small bowl until smooth; whisk into cooking liquid. Turn **CROCK-POT®** slow cooker to HIGH. Cook, uncovered, on HIGH 10 minutes or until thickened. Add carrots and return pork to **CROCK-POT®** slow cooker; mix well. Cover; cook on HIGH 15 to 30 minutes or until heated through. Place pork filling evenly into lettuce leaves; wrap to enclose.

Makes 20 wraps

Mu Shu Pork Wraps: Lightly spread prepared gluten-free plum sauce over small warm corn tortillas. Spoon pork filling and stir-fried vegetables evenly onto tortillas; wrap to enclose. Serve immediately. Makes about 20 wraps.

Pork Chops à l'Orange

2 tablespoons extra virgin olive oil

8 bone-in pork chops

⅓ cup orange juice

2 tablespoons clover honey

1 teaspoon salt

1 teaspoon packed brown sugar

1 teaspoon grated orange peel

¼ cup water

2 tablespoons cornstarch

Hot cooked wild rice

1. Heat oil in large skillet over medium-high heat. Add pork in batches; cook 5 to 7 minutes on each side or until browned.

2. Combine orange juice, honey, salt, brown sugar and orange peel in **CROCK-POT®** slow cooker. Add pork; turn to coat. Cover; cook on LOW 6 to 8 hours.

3. Transfer pork to warm plate. Stir water into cornstarch in small bowl until smooth. Whisk into cooking liquid. Cover; cook on LOW 15 minutes or until thickened. Serve sauce over pork and rice.

Makes 8 servings

Pork Loin Stuffed with Stone Fruits

- 1 boneless pork loin roast (about 4 pounds)*
- 1 teaspoon salt, divided
- 1 teaspoon black pepper, divided
- 2 tablespoons vegetable oil
- 2 tablespoons butter
- 1 onion, chopped
- ½ cup Madeira or Sherry wine

- 1½ cups dried stone fruits (½ cup *each* plums, peaches and apricots)
- 2 cloves garlic, minced
- ¼ teaspoon dried thyme
- 1 tablespoon olive oil

*Unless you have a 5-, 6- or 7-quart CROCK-POT® slow cooker, cut any roast larger than 2½ pounds in half so it cooks completely.

1. Coat **CROCK-POT®** slow cooker with nonstick cooking spray. Season pork with ¼ teaspoon salt and ½ teaspoon pepper. Heat vegetable oil in large skillet over medium-high heat. Add pork; cook 5 to 7 minutes or until browned on all sides. Remove to cutting board. Cover loosely with foil; let stand 10 to 15 minutes.

2. Melt butter in same skillet over medium heat. Add onion; cook and stir until translucent. Add Madeira; cook 2 to 3 minutes until mixture reduces slightly. Stir in dried fruit, garlic, remaining ¾ teaspoon salt, remaining ½ teaspoon pepper and thyme; cook 1 minute. Remove from heat.

3. Cut strings from roast, if necessary. Butterfly roast lengthwise (use sharp knife to cut meat; cut to within 1½ inches of edge). Spread roast flat on cutting board, browned side down. Spoon fruit mixture onto pork roast. Bring sides together to close roast. Slide kitchen string under roast and tie roast shut, allowing 2 inches between ties. If any fruit escapes, push back gently. Place roast in **CROCK-POT®** slow cooker. Pour olive oil over roast. Cover; cook on LOW 5 to 6 hours or on HIGH 2 to 3 hours.

4. Remove roast to cutting board. Cover loosely with foil; let stand 10 to 15 minutes. Pour cooking liquid into small saucepan; cook over high heat about 3 minutes to reduce sauce. Slice roast and serve with sauce.

Makes 8 to 10 servings

Tip: To butterfly a roast means to split the meat down the center without cutting all the way through. This allows the meat to be spread open so a filling can be added.

Pork Roast with Fruit Medley

1 cup water	1 cup dried apricots
½ cup kosher or coarse salt	1 cup dried plums
2 tablespoons sugar	1 cup dry red wine
1 teaspoon dried thyme	2 cloves garlic, minced
2 whole bay leaves	Juice of ½ lemon
1 boneless pork roast (about 4 pounds)*	
Olive oil	
2 cups green grapes	

*Unless you have a 5-, 6- or 7-quart **CROCK-POT**® slow cooker, cut any roast larger than 2½ pounds in half so it cooks completely.*

1. Combine water, salt, sugar, thyme and bay leaves in large resealable food storage bag. Add roast. Marinate overnight or up to 2 days in refrigerator, turning occasionally.

2. Remove roast from marinade; lightly pat dry. Heat oil in large skillet over medium heat. Add roast; cook 5 to 7 minutes or until browned on all sides. Transfer to **CROCK-POT**® slow cooker.

3. Add grapes, apricots, plums, wine, garlic and lemon juice to **CROCK-POT**® slow cooker; stir gently to combine. Cover; cook on LOW 7 to 9 hours or on HIGH 3 to 5 hours.

Makes 6 to 8 servings

Chinese Pork Tenderloin

2 pork tenderloins (about 2 pounds total), cut into 1-inch cubes

1 jar (15 ounces) gluten-free sweet and sour sauce

1 green bell pepper, cut into ½-inch pieces

1 red bell pepper, cut into ½-inch pieces

1 onion, thinly sliced

2 carrots, thinly sliced

1 tablespoon gluten-free soy sauce

½ teaspoon hot pepper sauce

Hot cooked rice

Sprigs fresh cilantro (optional)

Place pork, sweet and sour sauce, bell peppers, onion, carrots, soy sauce and hot pepper sauce into **CROCK-POT®** slow cooker; stir until blended. Cover; cook on LOW 6 to 7 hours or on HIGH 4 to 5 hours. Serve over rice. Garnish with cilantro.

Makes 8 servings

Gluten-Free Tip: Product formulations change frequently. Don't assume just because you have used a brand or product in the past it's necessarily gluten-free forever. Check labels each time before you purchase them.

Sweet and Spicy Pork Picadillo

1 tablespoon olive oil

1 yellow onion, diced

2 cloves garlic, minced

1 pound boneless pork country-style ribs, trimmed and cut into 1-inch cubes

1 can (about 14 ounces) diced tomatoes

3 tablespoons cider vinegar

2 chipotle peppers in adobo sauce, chopped*

½ cup raisins, chopped

½ teaspoon cumin

½ teaspoon ground cinnamon

Salt and black pepper

You may substitute dried chipotle peppers, soaked in warm water about 20 minutes to soften before chopping.

1. Heat oil in large skillet over medium-low heat. Add onion and garlic; cook and stir 4 minutes or until onion is translucent. Add pork; cook 5 to 7 minutes or until browned. Transfer to **CROCK-POT®** slow cooker.

2. Combine tomatoes, vinegar, chipotle peppers, raisins, cumin and cinnamon in medium bowl. Pour over pork. Cover; cook on LOW 5 hours or on HIGH 3 hours. Remove pork to cutting board; shred with two forks. Return to **CROCK-POT®** slow cooker. Cover; cook on HIGH 30 minutes. Season with salt and black pepper.

Makes 4 servings

Holiday Ham

1 **bone-in cooked ham (about 5 to 7 pounds), trimmed**

16 **whole cloves**

1 **cup water**

1½ **teaspoons vegetable oil**

1 **shallot, chopped**

1 **jar (12 ounces) cherry preserves or currant jelly**

¾ **cup dried orange-flavored cranberries or raisins**

½ **cup packed brown sugar**

½ **cup orange juice**

½ **teaspoon dry mustard**

1. Score ham. Place 1 clove in center of each diamond. Pour water into **CROCK-POT®** slow cooker; add ham. Cover; cook on LOW 5 to 6 hours or on HIGH 2½ to 3 hours.

2. Heat oil in small saucepan over medium-high heat. Add shallot; cook and stir 2 to 3 minutes or until translucent. Stir in preserves, cranberries, brown sugar, orange juice and mustard. Reduce heat to medium; cook until brown sugar is dissolved.

3. Remove ham from **CROCK-POT®** slow cooker; drain liquid. Transfer ham back to **CROCK-POT®** slow cooker; pour fruit sauce over ham. Cover; cook on HIGH 10 to 20 minutes or until fruit plumps.

Makes 12 to 14 servings

Mini Carnitas Tacos

1½ pounds boneless pork loin, cut into 1-inch cubes

1 onion, finely chopped

½ cup gluten-free chicken broth

1 tablespoon chili powder

2 teaspoons ground cumin

1 teaspoon dried oregano

½ teaspoon minced canned chipotle peppers in adobo sauce

½ cup pico de gallo

2 tablespoons chopped fresh cilantro

½ teaspoon salt

12 (6-inch) corn tortillas

¾ cup (3 ounces) shredded sharp Cheddar cheese

3 tablespoons sour cream

1. Combine pork, onion, broth, chili powder, cumin, oregano and chipotle peppers in **CROCK-POT®** slow cooker. Cover; cook on LOW 6 hours or on HIGH 3 hours. Pour off excess cooking liquid.

2. Remove pork to cutting board; shred with two forks. Return to **CROCK-POT®** slow cooker. Stir in pico de gallo, cilantro and salt. Cover; keep warm on LOW or WARM setting. Cut three circles from each tortilla with 2-inch biscuit cutter. Top each with pork, cheese and sour cream.

Makes 12 servings

Tip: Carnitas, or "little meats" in Spanish, are a festive way to spice up any gathering. Carnitas traditionally include a large amount of lard, but slow cooking makes the dish healthier by eliminating the need to add lard, oil or fat, while keeping the meat tender and delicious.

Boneless Pork Roast with Garlic

1 boneless pork rib roast (2 to
2½ pounds)
Salt and black pepper
3 tablespoons olive oil, divided
¼ cup chopped fresh rosemary

4 cloves garlic, minced
½ lemon, cut into ⅛- to ¼-inch slices
½ cup gluten-free chicken broth
¼ cup dry white wine

1. Season pork roast with salt and pepper. Combine 2 tablespoons oil, rosemary and garlic in small bowl. Rub into pork. Roll and tie pork snugly with kitchen string. Tuck lemon slices under string and into ends of roast.

2. Heat remaining 1 tablespoon oil in large skillet over medium heat. Add pork; cook 5 to 7 minutes on each side or until browned. Transfer to **CROCK-POT®** slow cooker.

3. Return skillet to heat. Add broth and wine; cook and stir to scrape up any browned bits from skillet. Pour over pork in **CROCK-POT®** slow cooker. Cover; cook on LOW 8 to 9 hours or on HIGH 3½ to 4 hours.

4. Remove roast to cutting board. Cover loosely with foil; let stand 10 to 15 minutes before removing kitchen string and slicing. Serve with juice from **CROCK-POT®** slow cooker.

Makes 4 to 6 servings

Fall-off-the-Bone BBQ Ribs

½ cup paprika

¼ cup sugar

¼ cup onion powder

1½ teaspoons salt

1½ teaspoons black pepper

2½ pounds baby back pork ribs, silver skin removed

1 can (20 ounces) gluten-free beef broth

1 quart gluten-free barbecue sauce

½ cup honey

Sesame seeds and fresh chopped chives (optional)

1. Preheat grill. Lightly oil grill grid. Combine paprika, sugar, onion powder, salt and pepper in small bowl; rub into ribs. Place ribs on prepared grid. Cook 3 minutes on each side or until ribs have grill marks.

2. Portion ribs into 3 to 4 sections; place in **CROCK-POT®** slow cooker. Pour broth over ribs. Cover; cook on HIGH 2 hours. Combine barbecue sauce and honey in large bowl; add to **CROCK-POT®** slow cooker. Cover; cook on HIGH 1½ hours. Garnish with sesame seeds and chives.

Makes 6 to 8 servings

Rosemary Pork with Red Wine Risotto

1 boneless pork loin (about 3 pounds)*

Salt and black pepper

2 tablespoons olive oil

3 sprigs fresh rosemary, plus additional for garnish

2 cups gluten-free chicken broth, divided

½ cup minced onion

2 tablespoons butter, divided

3 cloves garlic, minced

1 cup uncooked Arborio rice

1 cup dry red wine

¾ cup grated Parmesan cheese

*Unless you have a 5-, 6- or 7-quart CROCK-POT® slow cooker, cut any roast larger than 2½ pounds in half so it cooks completely.

1. Season pork with salt and pepper. Heat oil in large skillet over medium-high heat. Add 3 sprigs rosemary and pork; cook 5 to 7 minutes or until browned on all sides. Transfer roast and rosemary to **CROCK-POT®** slow cooker.

2. Add ¼ cup broth to skillet, stirring to scrape up any browned bits. Add onion, 1 tablespoon butter and garlic; cook and stir 4 minutes or until onion is translucent. Add rice to skillet; cook and stir 2 minutes or until rice just begins to brown. Stir in wine and remaining 1¾ cups broth. Pour mixture around roast in **CROCK-POT®** slow cooker.

3. Cover; cook on HIGH 3 to 4 hours, stirring occasionally, until roast reaches 160°F on thermometer inserted into center. Remove and discard rosemary. Remove roast to cutting board. Cover loosely with foil; let stand 10 to 15 minutes.

4. Stir remaining 1 tablespoon butter and cheese into rice. Serve risotto with roast. Garnish with additional rosemary.

Makes 4 to 6 servings

Southwestern Pork Chop Dinner

1 package (about 1 ounce) taco seasoning mix, divided

6 boneless pork chops (cut to 1-inch thickness)

1 tablespoon olive oil

1 can (about 14 ounces) diced tomatoes, drained

1 can (about 15 ounces) pinto or kidney beans, rinsed and drained

1 cup frozen corn, thawed

1 tablespoon water

1 tablespoon cornstarch

Sprigs fresh Italian parsley (optional)

1. Rub 2 tablespoons taco seasoning mix over both sides of pork chops. Heat oil in large skillet over medium heat. Add pork in batches; cook 5 to 7 minutes on each side or until browned.

2. Combine tomatoes, beans, corn and remaining taco seasoning mix in **CROCK-POT®** slow cooker; mix well. Place pork over bean mixture. Cover; cook on LOW 5 to 6 hours or on HIGH 2 to 3 hours or until internal temperature of pork reaches 145°F. Remove pork to serving plate; cover with foil to keep warm.

3. Stir water into cornstarch in small bowl until smooth. Whisk into bean mixture. Cover; cook on HIGH 10 minutes or until thickened. Serve with pork. Garnish with parsley.

Makes 6 servings

Gluten-Free Tip: Cornstarch is a fine, white powder made from the heart of corn kernels (the endosperm). Therefore, it's gluten-free and is used as a thickener instead of flour for this pork chop dinner.

Pork Chops with Dried Fruit and Onions

6 bone-in end-cut pork chops
(about 2½ pounds)

Salt and black pepper

3 tablespoons vegetable oil

2 onions, diced

2 cloves garlic, minced

¼ teaspoon dried sage

3 cups unsweetened unfiltered
apple juice

¾ cup quartered pitted dried plums

¾ cup chopped mixed dried fruit

1 whole bay leaf

1. Season pork chops with salt and pepper. Heat oil in large skillet over medium-high heat. Add pork in batches; cook 5 to 7 minutes on each side or until browned. Transfer to **CROCK-POT®** slow cooker.

2. Add onions to skillet. Reduce heat to medium; cook and stir until softened. Add garlic; cook 30 seconds. Sprinkle sage over mixture. Add apple juice, plums and mixed fruit; bring mixture to a boil. Reduce heat to low; simmer 3 minutes, stirring to scrape up any browned bits. Pour mixture over pork chops in **CROCK-POT®** slow cooker. Add bay leaf.

3. Cover; cook on LOW 3½ to 4 hours. Remove and discard bay leaf. Serve fruit and cooking liquid over pork.

Makes 6 servings

Italian Sausage with White Beans

1 pound gluten-free bulk pork Italian sausage

½ cup minced onion

2 cans (about 15 ounces *each*) cannellini or Great Northern beans, rinsed and drained

1 can (about 14 ounces) Italian seasoned diced tomatoes

1 teaspoon dried rosemary

½ cup grated Parmesan or Romano cheese

1. Coat inside of **CROCK-POT**® slow cooker with nonstick cooking spray. Heat large skillet over medium-high heat. Brown sausage and onion 6 to 8 minutes, stirring to break up meat. Drain fat.

2. Combine beans, tomatoes and rosemary in **CROCK-POT**® slow cooker. Stir in sausage mixture. Cover; cook on LOW 3 to 4 hours or on HIGH 1½ to 2 hours. Ladle into bowls; top with cheese.

Makes 4 servings

Posole

3 pounds pork tenderloin, cubed

3 cans (about 14 ounces *each*) white hominy, rinsed and drained*

1 cup gluten-free chili sauce

Hominy is corn that has been treated to remove the germ and hull. It can be found with canned vegetables or beans in most supermarkets.

Combine pork, hominy and chili sauce in **CROCK-POT®** slow cooker. Cover; cook on LOW 10 hours or on HIGH 5 hours.

Makes 8 servings

Harvest Ham Supper

6 carrots, cut into 2-inch pieces

3 medium sweet potatoes, quartered

1 to 1½ pounds boneless ham

1 cup maple syrup

Arrange carrots and sweet potatoes in bottom of **CROCK-POT®** slow cooker. Place ham on top of vegetables; top with syrup. Cover; cook on LOW 6 to 8 hours.

Makes 6 servings

Chorizo Chili

1 **pound ground beef**

8 **ounces bulk gluten-free raw chorizo sausage** *or* ½ **(15-ounce) package gluten-free raw chorizo sausage***

2 **cans (about 14 ounces** *each***) chili-style diced tomatoes**

1 **can (about 15 ounces) gluten-free chili beans in chili sauce**

Optional toppings: sour cream, fresh chives, shredded Cheddar cheese and sliced green onions

*Chorizo is a highly seasoned Mexican pork sausage.

Place beef, chorizo, tomatoes and beans in **CROCK-POT®** slow cooker; stir to break up meat. Cover; cook on LOW 7 hours. Skim off excess fat before serving. Top as desired.

Makes 6 servings

Vegetarian Chili

1 tablespoon vegetable oil

1 cup chopped onion

1 cup chopped red bell pepper

2 tablespoons minced jalapeño peppers*

1 clove garlic, minced

1 can (28 ounces) crushed tomatoes, undrained

1 can (about 15 ounces) black beans, rinsed and drained

1 can (about 15 ounces) chickpeas, rinsed and drained

½ cup frozen corn, thawed

¼ cup tomato paste

1 teaspoon sugar

1 teaspoon ground cumin

1 teaspoon dried basil

1 teaspoon chili powder

¼ teaspoon black pepper

*Jalapeño peppers can sting and irritate the skin, so wear rubber gloves when handling peppers and do not touch your eyes.

1. Heat oil in large skillet over medium-high heat. Add onion, bell pepper, jalapeño peppers and garlic; cook and stir 5 minutes or until tender. Transfer to **CROCK-POT®** slow cooker.

2. Add tomatoes, beans, chickpeas, corn, tomato paste, sugar, cumin, basil, chili powder and black pepper to **CROCK-POT®** slow cooker; mix well. Cover; cook on LOW 4 to 5 hours.

Makes 4 servings

Black Bean Mushroom Chili

1	tablespoon vegetable oil	1	can (about 14 ounces) fire-roasted diced tomatoes
2	cups (8 ounces) sliced baby bella or button mushrooms	1	cup salsa
1	cup chopped onion	1	yellow or green bell pepper, diced
4	cloves garlic, minced	2	teaspoons chili powder or ground cumin (or 1 teaspoon *each*)
1	can (about 15 ounces) black beans, rinsed and drained		Sour cream

1. Coat inside of **CROCK-POT®** slow cooker with nonstick cooking spray. Heat oil in large skillet over medium heat. Add mushrooms, onion and garlic; cook and stir 8 minutes or until mushrooms have released their liquid and liquid has thickened slightly.

2. Combine mushroom mixture, beans, tomatoes, salsa, bell pepper and chili powder in **CROCK-POT®** slow cooker; mix well. Cover; cook on LOW 5 to 6 hours or on HIGH 2½ to 3 hours. Ladle into bowls. Top with sour cream.

Makes 4 servings

Chicken and Black Bean Chili

1   **pound boneless, skinless chicken thighs, cut into 1-inch pieces**

2   **teaspoons chili powder**

2   **teaspoons ground cumin**

¾   **teaspoon salt**

1   **can (about 14 ounces) diced tomatoes**

1   **green bell pepper, diced**

1   **cup chunky salsa**

1   **small onion, chopped**

3   **cloves garlic, minced**

1   **can (about 15 ounces) black beans, rinsed and drained**

Optional toppings: sour cream, shredded Cheddar cheese and/ or sprigs fresh cilantro

Corn tortilla chips (optional)

1. Combine chicken, chili powder, cumin and salt in **CROCK-POT®** slow cooker; toss to coat.

2. Add tomatoes, bell pepper, salsa, onion and garlic; mix well. Cover; cook on LOW 5 to 6 hours or on HIGH 2½ to 3 hours.

3. Stir in beans. Cover; cook on HIGH 5 to 10 minutes or until heated through. Ladle into bowls. Top as desired. Serve with tortilla chips, if desired.

Makes 4 servings

Classic Chili

1½ pounds ground beef	2 to 3 teaspoons chili powder
1½ cups chopped onion	1 to 2 teaspoons ground mustard
1 cup chopped green bell pepper	¾ teaspoon dried basil
2 cloves garlic, minced	½ teaspoon black pepper
3 cans (about 15 ounces *each*) dark red kidney beans, rinsed and drained	1 to 2 dried red chiles (optional)
	Shredded Cheddar cheese (optional)
2 cans (about 15 ounces *each*) tomato sauce	Sprigs fresh Italian parsley (optional)
1 can (about 14 ounces) diced tomatoes	

1. Brown beef, onion, bell pepper and garlic 6 to 8 minutes in large skillet over medium-high heat, stirring to break up meat. Drain fat. Transfer beef mixture to **CROCK-POT®** slow cooker.

2. Add beans, tomato sauce, tomatoes, chili powder, mustard, basil, black pepper and chiles, if desired, to **CROCK-POT®** slow cooker; mix well. Cover; cook on LOW 8 to 10 hours or on HIGH 4 to 5 hours. Remove chiles before serving, if used.

Makes 6 servings

Tip: Slow-cooked recipes often provide a range of cooking times in order to account for variables, such as temperature of the ingredients before cooking, quantity of food in the **CROCK-POT®** slow cooker and the altitude.

Three-Bean Turkey Chili

1 pound ground turkey

1 small onion, chopped

1 can (28 ounces) diced tomatoes

1 can (about 15 ounces) chickpeas, rinsed and drained

1 can (about 15 ounces) kidney beans, rinsed and drained

1 can (about 15 ounces) black beans, rinsed and drained

1 can (8 ounces) gluten-free tomato sauce

1 can (4 ounces) diced mild green chiles

1 to 2 tablespoons chili powder

Sprigs fresh Italian parsley (optional)

1. Heat large skillet over medium-high heat. Add turkey and onion; cook and stir 6 to 8 minutes or until turkey is browned. Drain fat. Transfer to **CROCK-POT®** slow cooker.

2. Add tomatoes, chickpeas, beans, tomato sauce, chiles and chili powder to **CROCK-POT®** slow cooker; mix well. Cover; cook on HIGH 6 to 8 hours. Garnish with parsley.

Makes 6 to 8 servings

Kick'n Chili

2 pounds ground beef

2 cloves garlic, minced

1 tablespoon *each* salt, ground
   cumin, chili powder, paprika,
   dried oregano and black pepper

2 teaspoons red pepper flakes

¼ teaspoon ground red pepper

1 tablespoon vegetable oil

3 cans (about 14 ounces *each*)
   diced tomatoes with mild green
   chiles

1 jar (16 ounces) salsa

1 onion, chopped

Shredded Cheddar cheese
(optional)

Sour cream (optional)

1. Combine beef, garlic, salt, cumin, chili powder, paprika, oregano, black pepper, red pepper flakes and ground red pepper in large bowl.

2. Heat oil in large skillet over medium-high heat. Brown beef 6 to 8 minutes, stirring to break up meat. Drain fat. Add tomatoes, salsa and onion; mix well. Transfer to **CROCK-POT®** slow cooker.

3. Cover; cook on LOW 4 to 6 hours. Serve with cheese and sour cream, if desired.

Makes 6 servings

Tip: This chunky chili is perfect for the spicy food lover in your family. Reduce red pepper flakes for a milder flavor.

Three-Bean Chipotle Chili

2 tablespoons olive oil

1 onion, chopped

1 green bell pepper, chopped

2 cloves garlic, minced

2 cans (about 15 ounces *each*) pinto or pink beans, rinsed and drained

1 can (about 15 ounces) small white beans, rinsed and drained

1 can (about 15 ounces) chickpeas, rinsed and drained

1 cup frozen corn, thawed

1 cup water

1 can (6 ounces) tomato paste

1 or 2 canned chipotle peppers in adobo sauce, finely chopped

Salt and black pepper

Optional toppings: sour cream, shredded Cheddar cheese and/or fresh chopped chives

Corn tortilla chips (optional)

1. Heat oil in large skillet over medium heat. Add onion, bell pepper and garlic; cook and stir 3 to 5 minutes or until softened. Transfer to **CROCK-POT®** slow cooker.

2. Stir beans, chickpeas, corn, water, tomato paste and chipotle peppers into **CROCK-POT®** slow cooker. Cover; cook on LOW 3½ to 4 hours. Season with salt and black pepper. Top as desired. Serve with tortilla chips, if desired.

Makes 6 servings

Best Ever Chili

1½ pounds ground beef	1½ pounds plum tomatoes, diced
1 cup chopped onion	1 can (15 ounces) tomato paste
2 cans (about 15 ounces *each*) kidney beans, drained and 1 cup liquid reserved	3 to 6 tablespoons chili powder
	Sour cream
	Sliced green onions

1. Brown beef and onion 6 to 8 minutes in large skillet over medium-high heat, stirring to break up meat. Drain fat. Transfer beef and onion to **CROCK-POT®** slow cooker.

2. Add beans, reserved bean liquid, tomatoes, tomato paste and chili powder to **CROCK-POT®** slow cooker; mix well. Cover; cook on LOW 10 to 12 hours. Top with sour cream and green onions.

Makes 8 servings

Gluten-Free Tip: When you find a product marked gluten-free, you can be sure you are in safe territory. Wheat-free, however, is no guarantee. The product could contain gluten from barley, rye, oats or something derived from them. Remember wheat is considered an allergen and must be labeled. The others are not.

Chili Verde

Nonstick cooking spray

¾ pound boneless pork roast, cut into 1-inch cubes

1 pound fresh tomatillos, husks removed, coarsely chopped

1 can (about 15 ounces) Great Northern beans, rinsed and drained

1 can (about 14 ounces) gluten-free chicken broth

1 large onion, halved and thinly sliced

1 can (4 ounces) diced mild green chiles

6 cloves garlic, sliced

1 teaspoon ground cumin

Salt and black pepper

½ cup lightly packed fresh cilantro, chopped

1. Spray large skillet with cooking spray. Heat over medium-high heat. Add pork; cook and stir 5 to 7 minutes or until browned.

2. Combine pork, tomatillos, beans, broth, onion, chiles, garlic and cumin in **CROCK-POT®** slow cooker. Cover; cook on HIGH 3 to 4 hours.

3. Season with salt and pepper. Turn off heat. Stir in cilantro.

Makes 4 servings

Double-Hearty, Double-Quick Veggie Chili

2 cans (about 15 ounces *each*) dark kidney beans, rinsed and drained

1 package (16 ounces) frozen bell pepper stir-fry mixture, thawed *or* 2 bell peppers, chopped*

1 can (about 14 ounces) diced tomatoes with peppers, celery and onions

1 cup frozen corn, thawed

3 tablespoons chili powder

2 teaspoons sugar

2 teaspoons ground cumin, divided

1 tablespoon olive oil

½ teaspoon salt

Sour cream (optional)

Chopped fresh cilantro (optional)

If using fresh bell peppers, add 1 small onion, chopped.

Combine beans, bell pepper mixture, tomatoes, corn, chili powder, sugar and 1½ teaspoons cumin in **CROCK-POT®** slow cooker; mix well. Cover; cook on LOW 5 hours or on HIGH 3 hours. Stir in oil, salt and remaining ½ teaspoon cumin. Top with sour cream and cilantro, if desired.

Makes 4 to 6 servings

Black and White Chili

Nonstick cooking spray

1 pound chicken tenders, cut into ¾-inch pieces

1 cup coarsely chopped onion

1 can (about 15 ounces) Great Northern beans, rinsed and drained

1 can (about 15 ounces) black beans, rinsed and drained

1 can (about 14 ounces) Mexican-style stewed tomatoes, undrained

2 tablespoons Texas-style chili powder seasoning mix

1. Spray large skillet with cooking spray; heat over medium heat. Add chicken and onion; cook and stir 5 minutes or until chicken is browned.

2. Combine chicken mixture, beans, tomatoes and chili seasoning in **CROCK-POT®** slow cooker. Cover; cook on LOW 4 to 4½ hours.

Makes 6 servings

Serving Suggestion: For a change of pace, serve this delicious chili over cooked rice.

Corn and Two Bean Chili

1 can (about 15 ounces) pinto or kidney beans, rinsed and drained

1 can (about 15 ounces) black beans, rinsed and drained

1 can (about 14 ounces) fire-roasted diced tomatoes

1 cup salsa

1 cup frozen corn, thawed

½ cup minced onion

1 teaspoon chili powder

1 teaspoon ground cumin

½ cup sour cream (optional)

1 cup (4 ounces) shredded Cheddar cheese (optional)

Coat inside of **CROCK-POT**® slow cooker with nonstick cooking spray. Combine beans, tomatoes, salsa, corn, onion, chili powder and cumin in **CROCK-POT**® slow cooker; mix well. Cover; cook on LOW 5 to 6 hours or on HIGH 2½ to 3 hours. Ladle into bowls. Top with sour cream and cheese, if desired.

Makes 4 servings

Mediterranean Chili

2 cans (about 28 ounces *each*) chickpeas, rinsed and drained

1 can (28 ounces) chopped tomatoes

1 can (about 14 ounces) gluten-free vegetable broth

2 onions, chopped

10 kalamata olives, chopped

4 cloves garlic, chopped

2 teaspoons cumin

¼ teaspoon ground red pepper

½ cup chopped fresh mint

1 teaspoon oregano

½ teaspoon grated lemon peel

1 cup crumbled feta cheese

Sprigs fresh mint (optional)

Combine chickpeas, tomatoes, broth, onions, olives, garlic, cumin and ground red pepper in **CROCK-POT®** slow cooker. Cover; cook on LOW 7 to 8 hours or on HIGH 3½ hours. Stir in chopped mint, oregano and lemon peel. Ladle into bowls. Top with feta. Garnish with mint sprigs.

Makes 6 servings

Tip: Keep the lid on! The **CROCK-POT®** slow cooker can take as long as 30 minutes to regain heat lost when the cover is removed. Only remove the cover when instructed to do so by the recipe.

White Bean Chili

Nonstick cooking spray

1 pound ground chicken

1 can (28 ounces) whole tomatoes, undrained and coarsely chopped

3 cups coarsely chopped celery

1 can (about 15 ounces) Great Northern beans, rinsed and drained

1½ cups coarsely chopped onions

1 cup gluten-free chicken broth

3 cloves garlic, minced

1 tablespoon plus 1 teaspoon chili powder

1½ teaspoons ground cumin

¾ teaspoon ground allspice

¾ teaspoon ground cinnamon

½ teaspoon black pepper

1. Spray large skillet with cooking spray; heat over medium-high heat. Add chicken; cook and stir 5 to 7 minutes or until browned.

2. Combine chicken, tomatoes, celery, beans, onions, broth, garlic, chili powder, cumin, allspice, cinnamon and pepper in **CROCK-POT®** slow cooker. Cover; cook on LOW 5½ to 6 hours.

Makes 6 servings

Chili with Turkey and Beans

2 cans (about 15 ounces *each*) red kidney beans, rinsed and drained

2 cans (about 14 ounces *each*) whole tomatoes, drained

1 pound cooked ground turkey

1 can (about 15 ounces) black beans, rinsed and drained

1 can (12 ounces) tomato sauce

1 cup finely chopped onion

1 cup finely chopped celery

1 cup finely chopped carrot

½ cup amaretto (optional)

3 tablespoons chili powder

1 tablespoon plus 1 teaspoon ground cumin

1 tablespoon gluten-free Worcestershire sauce

2 teaspoons ground red pepper

1 teaspoon salt

Shredded Cheddar cheese (optional)

Combine kidney beans, tomatoes, turkey, black beans, tomato sauce, onion, celery, carrot, amaretto, if desired, chili powder, cumin, Worcestershire sauce, ground red pepper and salt in **CROCK-POT®** slow cooker. Cover; cook on HIGH 7 hours. Top with cheese, if desired.

Makes 4 servings

Hearty Chicken Chili

2 cans (about 15 ounces *each*) hominy, rinsed and drained*

1½ pounds boneless, skinless chicken thighs, cut into 1-inch pieces

1 can (about 15 ounces) pinto beans, rinsed and drained

1 cup gluten-free chicken broth

1 medium onion, finely chopped

1 small jalapeño pepper, seeded and minced**

1 clove garlic, minced

1½ teaspoons chili powder

¾ teaspoon salt

½ teaspoon ground cumin

½ teaspoon dried oregano

½ teaspoon black pepper

Chopped fresh Italian parsley or cilantro (optional)

Hominy is corn that has been treated to remove the germ and hull. It can be found with the canned vegetables or beans in most supermarkets.

**Jalapeño peppers can sting and irritate the skin, so wear rubber gloves when handling peppers and do not touch your eyes.*

Stir hominy, chicken, beans, broth, onion, jalapeño pepper, garlic, chili powder, salt, cumin, oregano and black pepper in **CROCK-POT®** slow cooker. Cover; cook on LOW 7 hours. Garnish with parsley.

Makes 6 servings

Weeknight Chili

- 1 **pound ground beef or turkey**
- 1 **package (about 1 ounce) chili seasoning mix**
- 1 **can (about 15 ounces) red kidney beans, rinsed and drained**
- 1 **can (about 14 ounces) diced tomatoes with mild green chiles**
- 1 **can (8 ounces) tomato sauce**
- 1 **cup (4 ounces) shredded Cheddar cheese (optional)**

Sliced green onions (optional)

1. Brown beef 6 to 8 minutes in large skillet over medium-high heat, stirring to break up meat. Drain fat. Stir in seasoning mix.

2. Place beef mixture, beans, tomatoes and tomato sauce in **CROCK-POT®** slow cooker. Cover; cook on LOW 4 to 6 hours or on HIGH 2 to 3 hours. Top with cheese and green onions, if desired.

Makes 4 servings

Slow-Roasted Potatoes

16 small new red potatoes, unpeeled
3 tablespoons butter, cubed
1 teaspoon paprika
½ teaspoon salt
¼ teaspoon garlic powder
Black pepper
1 to 2 tablespoons water

Combine potatoes, butter, paprika, salt, garlic powder and pepper in **CROCK-POT®** slow cooker; mix well. Cover; cook on LOW 7 hours or on HIGH 4 hours. Remove potatoes with slotted spoon to serving dish; keep warm. Add water to cooking liquid; stir until well blended. Pour over potatoes.

Makes 3 to 4 servings

Wild Rice and Dried Cherry Risotto

1 cup dry-roasted salted peanuts

6 teaspoons sesame oil, divided

1 cup chopped onion

4 cups hot water

6 ounces uncooked wild rice

1 cup diced carrots

1 cup chopped green or red bell pepper

½ cup dried cherries

⅛ to ¼ teaspoon red pepper flakes

¼ cup gluten-free teriyaki or soy sauce

1 teaspoon salt

1. Coat inside of **CROCK-POT®** slow cooker with nonstick cooking spray. Heat large skillet over medium-high heat. Add peanuts; cook and stir 2 to 3 minutes or until golden brown. Remove nuts to plate; set aside.

2. Heat 2 teaspoons oil in same skillet. Add onion; cook and stir 6 minutes or until browned. Transfer to **CROCK-POT®** slow cooker.

3. Stir in water, rice, carrots, bell pepper, cherries and red pepper flakes. Cover; cook on HIGH 3 hours.

4. Turn off heat. Let stand 15 minutes, uncovered, until rice absorbs liquid. Stir in teriyaki sauce, peanuts, remaining 4 teaspoons oil and salt.

Makes 8 to 10 servings

Cheese Grits with Chiles and Bacon

6 slices bacon

1 serrano or jalapeño pepper, seeded and minced*

1 large shallot or small onion, finely chopped

4 cups gluten-free chicken broth

1 cup grits**

Salt and black pepper

1 cup (4 ounces) shredded Cheddar cheese

½ cup half-and-half

2 tablespoons finely chopped green onion

Serrano peppers can sting and irritate the skin, so wear rubber gloves when handling peppers and do not touch your eyes.

**Use coarse, instant, yellow or stone-ground grits.*

1. Heat large skillet over medium heat. Add bacon; cook and stir until crisp. Remove to paper towel-lined plate using slotted spoon. Cut 2 strips into bite-size pieces; place in **CROCK-POT®** slow cooker. Refrigerate remaining 4 strips of bacon until ready to serve.

2. Drain all but 1 tablespoon bacon drippings from skillet. Add serrano pepper and shallot to skillet; cook and stir over medium-high heat 1 minute or until shallot is lightly browned. Transfer to **CROCK-POT®** slow cooker. Stir broth, grits, salt and black pepper into **CROCK-POT®** slow cooker. Cover; cook on LOW 4 hours.

3. Stir in cheese and half-and-half. Chop remaining bacon into bite-size pieces; sprinkle on top of each serving. Sprinkle with green onion.

Makes 4 servings

Orange-Spice Glazed Carrots

1 package (32 ounces) baby carrots

½ cup packed light brown sugar

½ cup orange juice

3 tablespoons butter

¾ teaspoon ground cinnamon

¼ teaspoon ground nutmeg

¼ cup cold water

2 tablespoons cornstarch

Chopped fresh basil (optional)

Orange peel twists (optional)

1. Combine carrots, brown sugar, orange juice, butter, cinnamon and nutmeg in **CROCK-POT®** slow cooker. Cover; cook on LOW 3½ to 4 hours.

2. Spoon carrots into serving bowl. Turn **CROCK-POT®** slow cooker to HIGH. Stir water into cornstarch in small bowl until smooth. Whisk into cooking liquid. Cover; cook on HIGH 5 to 10 minutes or until thickened. Spoon over carrots. Garnish with basil and orange twists.

Makes 6 servings

On the Side

Burgundy and Wild Cremini Mushroom Pilaf

2 tablespoons vegetable oil

2 cups uncooked converted long grain rice

1 medium onion, chopped

1 cup sliced wild cremini mushrooms

1 small zucchini, thinly sliced

3½ cups gluten-free beef or vegetable broth

½ cup dry burgundy or other dry red wine

¼ cup (½ stick) butter, melted

½ teaspoon salt

¼ teaspoon black pepper

1. Heat oil in large skillet over medium heat. Add rice, onion, mushrooms and zucchini; cook and stir 4 to 5 minutes or until rice is slightly browned and onions are soft. Transfer to **CROCK-POT®** slow cooker.

2. Add broth, burgundy, butter, salt and pepper; stir once. Cover; cook on LOW 6 to 8 hours.

Makes 6 servings

Tip: To make cleanup easier, spray the inside of the **CROCK-POT®** slow cooker with nonstick cooking spray before adding ingredients.

Spanish Paella-Style Rice

2 cans (about 14 ounces *each*) gluten-free vegetable broth

1½ cups uncooked converted long grain rice

1 small red bell pepper, chopped

⅓ cup dry white wine or water

½ teaspoon saffron threads, crushed, *or* ½ teaspoon ground turmeric

⅛ teaspoon red pepper flakes

½ cup frozen peas, thawed

Salt

1. Combine broth, rice, bell pepper, wine, saffron and red pepper flakes in **CROCK-POT®** slow cooker; mix well. Cover; cook on LOW 4 hours or until liquid is absorbed.

2. Stir in peas. Turn **CROCK-POT®** slow cooker to HIGH. Cover; cook on HIGH 15 to 30 minutes or until peas are heated through. Season with salt.

Makes 6 servings

Simmered Napa Cabbage with Dried Apricots

4 cups napa cabbage or green cabbage, cored and thinly sliced

1 cup chopped dried apricots

¼ cup clover honey

2 tablespoons orange juice

½ cup dry red wine

Salt and black pepper

Grated orange peel (optional)

1. Combine cabbage and apricots in **CROCK-POT®** slow cooker; toss well.

2. Combine honey and orange juice in small bowl; stir until smooth. Drizzle over cabbage. Add wine. Cover; cook on LOW 5 to 6 hours or on HIGH 2 to 3 hours or until cabbage is tender. Season with salt and pepper. Garnish with orange peel.

Makes 4 servings

Tip: Napa cabbage, also known as Chinese cabbage, is a loosely packed elongated head of light green stalks that are slightly crinkled. This variety has a milder flavor and doesn't give off a strong odor when cooked.

Rustic Cheddar Mashed Potatoes

2 pounds russet potatoes, diced
1 cup water
⅓ cup butter, cubed
½ to ¾ cup milk
1¼ teaspoons salt

½ teaspoon black pepper
¾ cup (3 ounces) shredded Cheddar cheese
½ cup finely chopped green onions

1. Combine potatoes and water in **CROCK-POT®** slow cooker; dot with butter. Cover; cook on LOW 6 hours or on HIGH 3 hours.

2. Transfer potatoes to large bowl. Beat potatoes with electric mixer at medium speed 3 to 5 minutes or until creamy. Add milk, salt and pepper; beat until smooth. Stir in cheese and green onions. Cover; let stand 15 minutes or until cheese is melted.

Makes 8 servings

Parmesan Potato Wedges

2 **pounds red potatoes, unpeeled and cut into ½-inch wedges**	½ **teaspoon salt**
¼ **cup finely chopped yellow onion**	¼ **teaspoon black pepper**
1½ **teaspoons dried oregano**	2 **tablespoons butter, cubed**
	¼ **cup grated Parmesan cheese**

Layer potatoes, onion, oregano, salt and pepper in **CROCK-POT®** slow cooker; dot with butter. Cover; cook on HIGH 4 hours. Remove potatoes to serving platter; sprinkle with cheese.

Makes 6 servings

Lemon and Tangerine Glazed Carrots

6 cups sliced carrots

1½ cups apple juice

¼ cup (½ stick) plus 2 tablespoons butter

¼ cup packed brown sugar

2 tablespoons grated lemon peel

2 tablespoons grated tangerine peel

½ teaspoon salt

Chopped fresh Italian parsley (optional)

Combine carrots, apple juice, butter, brown sugar, lemon peel, tangerine peel and salt in **CROCK-POT®** slow cooker. Cover; cook on LOW 4 to 5 hours or on HIGH 1 to 3 hours. Garnish with parsley.

Makes 10 to 12 servings

Southwestern Corn and Beans

1 tablespoon olive oil

1 large onion, diced

1 or 2 jalapeño peppers, diced*

1 clove garlic, minced

2 cans (about 15 ounces *each*) kidney beans, rinsed and drained

1 bag (16 ounces) frozen corn, thawed

1 can (about 14 ounces) diced tomatoes

1 green bell pepper, cut into 1-inch pieces

2 teaspoons chili powder

¾ teaspoon salt

½ teaspoon ground cumin

½ teaspoon black pepper

Sour cream or plain yogurt (optional)

Sliced black olives (optional)

Jalapeño peppers can sting and irritate the skin, so wear rubber gloves when handling peppers and do not touch your eyes.

1. Heat oil in medium skillet over medium heat. Add onion, jalapeño pepper and garlic; cook and stir 5 minutes.

2. Combine onion mixture, beans, corn, tomatoes, bell pepper, chili powder, salt, cumin and black pepper in **CROCK-POT®** slow cooker; mix well. Cover; cook on LOW 7 to 8 hours or on HIGH 2 to 3 hours. Serve with sour cream and black olives, if desired.

Makes 6 servings

Serving Suggestion: Spoon this colorful side dish into hollowed-out bell peppers.

Supper Squash Medley

2 **butternut squash, peeled, seeded and diced**

1 **can (28 ounces) diced tomatoes**

1 **can (15 ounces) corn, drained**

2 **onions, chopped**

2 **green bell peppers, chopped**

1 **cup gluten-free chicken broth**

2 **teaspoons minced garlic**

2 **canned mild green chiles, chopped**

1 **teaspoon salt**

½ **teaspoon black pepper**

1 **can (6 ounces) tomato paste**

Sprig fresh basil (optional)

1. Combine squash, tomatoes, corn, onions, bell peppers, broth, garlic, chiles, salt and black pepper in **CROCK-POT®** slow cooker. Cover; cook on LOW 6 hours.

2. Remove about ½ cup cooking liquid and blend with tomato paste in small bowl. Return to **CROCK-POT®** slow cooker; stir well. Cover; cook on LOW 30 minutes or until mixture is slightly thickened and heated through. Garnish with basil.

Makes 8 to 10 servings

Lemon Dilled Parsnips and Turnips

4 turnips, cut into ½-inch pieces
3 parsnips, cut into ½-inch pieces
2 cups gluten-free chicken broth
¼ cup chopped green onions
¼ cup lemon juice
¼ cup dried dill

1 teaspoon minced garlic
¼ cup cold water
2 tablespoons cornstarch
  Lemon peel twists and green onion tops (optional)

1. Combine turnips, parsnips, broth, chopped green onions, lemon juice, dill and garlic in **CROCK-POT**® slow cooker; mix well. Cover; cook on LOW 3 to 4 hours or on HIGH 1 to 3 hours.

2. Stir water into cornstarch in small bowl until smooth. Whisk into **CROCK-POT**® slow cooker. Cover; cook on HIGH 15 minutes or until thickened. Garnish with lemon twists and green onion tops.

Makes 8 to 10 servings

Gratin Potatoes with Asiago Cheese

6 slices bacon, cut into 1-inch pieces

6 medium baking potatoes, thinly sliced

½ cup grated Asiago cheese

Salt and black pepper

1½ cups heavy cream

1. Heat large skillet over medium heat. Add bacon; cook and stir until crisp. Transfer to paper towel-lined plate using slotted spoon.

2. Pour bacon drippings into **CROCK-POT®** slow cooker. Layer one fourth of potatoes on bottom of **CROCK-POT®** slow cooker. Sprinkle one fourth of bacon over potatoes and top with one fourth of cheese. Season with salt and pepper. Repeat layers three more times. Pour cream over all. Cover; cook on LOW 7 to 9 hours or on HIGH 5 to 6 hours.

Makes 4 to 6 servings

Tip: Store uncooked potatoes in a cool, dark, dry, well-ventilated place. Do not refrigerate potatoes. It's important to protect them from light, because it can cause them to turn green and lose quality.

Mexican-Style Spinach

3 packages (10 ounces *each*) frozen chopped spinach, thawed

1 tablespoon canola oil

1 onion, chopped

1 clove garlic, minced

2 Anaheim peppers, roasted, peeled and minced*

3 fresh tomatillos, roasted, husks removed and chopped**

*Anaheim peppers can sting and irritate the skin, so wear rubber gloves when handling peppers and do not touch your eyes. To roast, heat skillet over medium heat. Add Anaheim peppers, cook and turn often until skins are brown and interior flesh is soft. Remove from skillet. Mince when cool enough to handle.

**To roast tomatillos, heat skillet over medium heat. Add tomatillos; cook and turn often until husks are brown and interior flesh is soft. Remove from skillet. Remove and discard husks when cool enough to handle.

Place spinach in **CROCK-POT®** slow cooker. Heat oil in large skillet over medium heat. Add onion and garlic; cook and stir 5 minutes or until onion is soft but not browned. Add Anaheim peppers and tomatillos; cook and stir 3 to 4 minutes. Add mixture to **CROCK-POT®** slow cooker. Cover; cook on LOW 4 to 6 hours.

Makes 6 servings

Pesto Rice and Beans

1 can (about 15 ounces) Great Northern beans, rinsed and drained

1 can (about 14 ounces) gluten-free vegetable broth

¾ cup uncooked converted long grain rice

1½ cups frozen cut green beans, thawed and drained

½ cup prepared pesto

Grated Parmesan cheese

1. Combine Great Northern beans, broth and rice in **CROCK-POT**® slow cooker. Cover; cook on LOW 2 hours.

2. Stir in green beans. Cover; cook on LOW 1 hour or until rice and beans are tender.

3. Turn off heat. Transfer **CROCK-POT**® stoneware to heatproof surface. Stir in pesto and cheese. Cover; let stand 5 minutes or until cheese is melted.

Makes 8 servings

New England Baked Beans

3 cans (about 15 ounces each) Great Northern beans, rinsed and drained

¾ cup water

4 slices bacon, crisp-cooked and chopped

1 small onion, chopped

⅓ cup canned diced tomatoes

3 tablespoons packed light brown sugar

3 tablespoons maple syrup

3 tablespoons molasses

2 cloves garlic, minced

½ teaspoon salt

½ teaspoon dry mustard

⅛ teaspoon black pepper

1 whole bay leaf

Combine beans, water, bacon, onion, tomatoes, brown sugar, maple syrup, molasses, garlic, salt, dry mustard, pepper and bay leaf in **CROCK-POT®** slow cooker. Cover; cook on LOW 6 to 8 hours. Remove and discard bay leaf.

Makes 4 to 6 servings

Orange-Spiced Sweet Potatoes

2 **pounds sweet potatoes, diced**	½ **teaspoon ground nutmeg**
½ **cup packed dark brown sugar**	½ **teaspoon grated orange peel**
½ **cup (1 stick) butter, cubed**	**Chopped toasted pecans***
Juice of 1 medium orange	
1 **teaspoon ground cinnamon**	**To toast pecans, spread in single layer in*
1 **teaspoon vanilla**	*heavy skillet. Cook over medium heat 1 to*
½ **teaspoon salt**	*2 minutes or until nuts are lightly browned, stirring frequently.*

Place sweet potatoes, brown sugar, butter, orange juice, cinnamon, vanilla, salt, nutmeg and orange peel in **CROCK-POT®** slow cooker. Cover; cook on LOW 4 hours or on HIGH 2 hours. Sprinkle with pecans.

Makes 8 servings

Variation: For a creamy variation, add ¼ cup milk or whipping cream. Beat potatoes with electric mixer at medium speed 3 to 5 minutes or until creamy. Sprinkle with cinnamon-sugar and pecans.

Creamy Red Pepper Polenta

6 cups boiling water

2 cups yellow cornmeal

1 small red bell pepper, finely chopped

¼ cup (½ stick) butter, melted

¼ teaspoon paprika, plus additional for garnish

⅛ teaspoon ground red pepper

⅛ teaspoon ground cumin

2 teaspoons salt

Red bell pepper strips (optional)

Combine water, cornmeal, chopped bell pepper, butter, ¼ teaspoon paprika, ground red pepper, cumin and salt in **CROCK-POT®** slow cooker; stir well to combine. Cover; cook on LOW 3 to 4 hours or on HIGH 1 to 2 hours, stirring occasionally. Garnish with additional paprika and bell pepper strips.

Makes 4 to 6 servings

Risotto-Style Peppered Rice

1 cup uncooked converted long grain rice

1 medium green bell pepper, chopped

1 medium red bell pepper, chopped

1 cup chopped onion

½ teaspoon ground turmeric

⅛ teaspoon ground red pepper (optional)

1 can (about 14 ounces) gluten-free vegetable broth

4 ounces Monterey Jack cheese with jalapeño peppers, cubed

½ cup milk

1 cup (2 sticks) butter, cubed

1 teaspoon salt

1. Place rice, bell peppers, onion, turmeric and ground red pepper, if desired, in **CROCK-POT®** slow cooker. Stir in broth. Cover; cook on LOW 4 to 5 hours or until rice is tender and broth is absorbed.

2. Stir in cheese, milk, butter and salt; fluff rice with fork. Cover; cook on LOW 5 to 10 minutes or until cheese is melted.

Makes 4 to 6 servings

Tip: Dairy products should be added at the end of the cooking time, because they will curdle if cooked in the **CROCK-POT®** slow cooker for a long time.

Carne Rellenos

1 **can (4 ounces) whole mild green chiles, drained**	1 **beef flank steak (about 2 pounds)**
4 **ounces cream cheese, softened**	1½ **cups salsa verde**
	Hot cooked rice

1. Slit whole chiles open on one side with sharp knife; stuff with cream cheese.

2. Open steak flat on sheet of waxed paper. Score steak; turn over. Lay stuffed chiles across unscored side of steak. Roll up; tie with kitchen string.

3. Place steak in **CROCK-POT®** slow cooker; pour in salsa. Cover; cook on LOW 6 to 8 hours or on HIGH 3 to 4 hours. Serve steak over rice with sauce.

Makes 6 servings

Slow Cooker Pepper Steak

2 tablespoons vegetable oil

3 pounds boneless beef top sirloin steak, cut into strips

1 tablespoon minced garlic (5 to 6 cloves)

1 medium onion, chopped

½ cup gluten-free soy sauce

2 teaspoons sugar

1 teaspoon salt

½ teaspoon ground ginger

½ teaspoon black pepper

3 green bell peppers, cut into strips

¼ cup cold water

1 tablespoon cornstarch

Hot cooked rice

1. Heat oil in large skillet over medium heat. Add steak strips in batches; cook and stir 6 to 8 minutes or until browned. Add garlic; cook and stir 2 minutes. Transfer steak strips, garlic and pan juices to **CROCK-POT®** slow cooker.

2. Add onion, soy sauce, sugar, salt, ginger and black pepper to **CROCK-POT®** slow cooker; mix well. Cover; cook on LOW 8 to 10 hours. Add bell peppers during final hour of cooking.

3. Stir water into cornstarch in small bowl until smooth. Whisk into **CROCK-POT®** slow cooker. Turn **CROCK-POT®** slow cooker to HIGH. Cook, uncovered, on HIGH 15 minutes or until thickened. Serve with rice.

Makes 6 to 8 servings

Gluten-Free Tip: Traditional Chinese soy sauce is brewed from soybeans and wheat, so it's off limits. There are some brands that skip the brewing process and use soy concentrate and caramel coloring instead. The good news is that these gluten-free soy sauces are cheaper, but they do lack flavor and complexity.

Maple Whiskey-Glazed Beef Brisket

1 teaspoon ground red pepper

1 tablespoon coarse salt

½ teaspoon black pepper

1½ to 2 pounds beef brisket, scored with a knife on both sides

½ cup maple syrup

Juice of 1 orange

¼ cup whiskey

2 tablespoons packed brown sugar

2 tablespoons olive oil

1 tablespoon tomato paste

2 cloves garlic, crushed

4 slices (¹⁄₁₆-inch-thick *each*) fresh ginger

4 slices (½×1½-inch thick *each*) orange peel

1. Combine ground red pepper, salt and black pepper in small bowl. Rub over brisket. Place brisket in large resealable food storage bag; set aside.

2. Combine syrup, orange juice, whiskey, brown sugar, oil, tomato paste, garlic, ginger and orange peel in medium bowl; stir until blended. Pour mixture over brisket in resealable storage bag. Refrigerate brisket 2 hours or overnight.

3. Transfer brisket and marinade to **CROCK-POT®** slow cooker. Cover, cook on LOW 7 to 9 hours, turning brisket once or twice. Slice thinly across the grain to serve.

Makes 4 to 6 servings

Portuguese Madeira Beef Shanks

1 large white onion, diced

1 green bell pepper, diced

½ cup diced celery

½ cup minced fresh Italian parsley

4 cloves garlic, minced

2 jalapeño peppers, seeded and minced*

4 medium bone-in beef shanks, (about 3 pounds total)

1 tablespoon fresh rosemary, minced

1 teaspoon salt

1 cup gluten-free beef broth

1 cup dry Madeira wine

Hot cooked rice (optional)

Sprigs fresh Italian parsley (optional)

Jalapeño peppers can sting and irritate the skin, so wear rubber gloves when handling peppers and do not touch your eyes.

1. Place onion, bell pepper, celery, minced parsley, garlic and jalapeño peppers in **CROCK-POT®** slow cooker.

2. Rub beef shanks with rosemary and salt; place on top of vegetables. Pour broth and wine over shanks and vegetables.

3. Cover; cook on LOW 7 to 9 hours. Top shanks with vegetable sauce. Serve with rice, if desired. Garnish with parsley sprigs.

Makes 4 servings

Merlot Beef and Sun-Dried Tomato Portobello Ragoût

1 jar (7 ounces) sun-dried tomatoes, packed in oil, drained and 3 tablespoons oil reserved

1 boneless beef chuck roast (about 3 pounds), cut into 1½-inch pieces

1 can (10½ ounces) gluten-free beef consommé, undiluted

6 ounces sliced portobello mushrooms

1 medium green bell pepper, cut into thin strips

1 medium orange or yellow bell pepper, cut into thin strips

1 medium onion, cut into 8 wedges

2 teaspoons dried oregano
Salt

¼ teaspoon garlic powder

½ cup Merlot or other dry red wine

2 tablespoons gluten-free Worcestershire sauce

1 tablespoon cornstarch

1 tablespoon balsamic vinegar
Black pepper
Hot cooked mashed potatoes

1. Heat 1 tablespoon reserved oil in large skillet over medium-high heat. Add one third of beef; brown on all sides. Transfer to **CROCK-POT**® slow cooker. Repeat with remaining oil and beef.

2. Add consommé to skillet; cook and stir to scrape up any browned bits. Pour mixture over beef. Add sun-dried tomatoes, mushrooms, bell peppers, onion, oregano, salt and garlic powder to **CROCK-POT**® slow cooker.

3. Combine Merlot and Worcestershire sauce in small bowl; reserve ¼ cup. Gently stir remaining Merlot mixture into **CROCK-POT**® slow cooker. Cover; cook on LOW 8 to 9 hours or on HIGH 4 to 5 hours.

4. Stir cornstarch and vinegar into reserved ¼ cup Merlot mixture until cornstarch is dissolved. Whisk into **CROCK-POT**® slow cooker. Cover; cook on HIGH 15 minutes or until thickened slightly. Season with black pepper. Serve over mashed potatoes.

Makes 8 servings

Tip: Consommé is just clarified broth. If you cannot find canned beef consommé, you may substitute beef broth.

Asian Beef with Broccoli

1½ pounds boneless beef chuck roast (about 1½ inches thick), sliced into thin strips*

1 can (10½ ounces) gluten-free condensed beef consommé, undiluted

½ cup gluten-free oyster sauce

2 tablespoons cornstarch

2 cups frozen broccoli, thawed

Hot cooked rice

Sesame seeds (optional)

*Freezing roast 30 minutes will make slicing easier.

1. Place beef in **CROCK-POT®** slow cooker. Pour consommé and oyster sauce over beef. Cover; cook on HIGH 3 hours.

2. Stir 2 tablespoons cooking liquid into cornstarch in small bowl until smooth. Whisk into **CROCK-POT®** slow cooker. Cover; cook on HIGH 10 to 15 minutes until thickened.

3. Add broccoli to **CROCK-POT®** slow cooker; toss gently to mix. Serve over rice. Garnish with sesame seeds.

Makes 4 to 6 servings

Horseradish Roast Beef and Potatoes

3 pounds beef roast*

1 teaspoon dried thyme, basil or oregano

1 tablespoon minced fresh Italian parsley

1 tablespoon freshly grated horseradish

1 tablespoon Dijon mustard

1 to 2 pounds Yukon Gold potatoes, quartered

2 cans (about 14 ounces *each*) gluten-free beef broth

1 pound mushrooms, cut into pieces

2 large tomatoes, seeded and diced

1 large onion, sliced

1 green bell pepper, chopped

1 red bell pepper, chopped

1 cup dry red wine

3 cloves garlic, minced

1 whole bay leaf

Salt and black pepper

*Unless you have a 5-, 6- or 7-quart **CROCK-POT**® slow cooker, cut any roast larger than 2½ pounds in half so it cooks completely.*

1. Place roast in **CROCK-POT**® slow cooker. Combine thyme, parsley, horseradish and Dijon mustard in small bowl; stir to make a paste. Spread paste over roast.

2. Add potatoes, broth, mushrooms, tomatoes, onion, bell peppers, wine, garlic, bay leaf, salt and black pepper to **CROCK-POT**® slow cooker. Add enough water to cover roast and vegetables. Cover; cook on HIGH 2 hours. Turn **CROCK-POT**® slow cooker to LOW. Cover; cook on LOW 4 to 6 hours. Remove and discard bay leaf.

Makes 12 servings

Shepherd's Pie

1 pound ground beef

1 pound ground lamb

1 package (12 ounces) frozen chopped onions, thawed

2 teaspoons minced garlic

1 package (16 ounces) frozen peas and carrots, thawed

1 can (about 14 ounces) diced tomatoes, drained

3 tablespoons quick-cooking tapioca

2 teaspoons dried oregano

1 teaspoon salt

½ teaspoon black pepper

3 cups hot cooked mashed potatoes

1. Brown beef and lamb 6 to 8 minutes in large skillet over medium-high heat, stirring to break up meat. Drain fat. Transfer to **CROCK-POT®** slow cooker. Return skillet to heat. Add onions and garlic; cook and stir until onions are tender. Transfer to **CROCK-POT®** slow cooker.

2. Stir peas and carrots, tomatoes, tapioca, oregano, salt and pepper into **CROCK-POT®** slow cooker. Cover; cook on LOW 7 to 8 hours. Top with mashed potatoes. Cover; cook on LOW 30 minutes or until potatoes are heated through.

Makes 6 servings

Italian Braised Short Ribs in Red Wine

3 pounds beef short ribs, trimmed
Salt and black pepper
1 tablespoon vegetable oil, plus additional as needed
2 onions, sliced
2 packages (8 ounces *each*) cremini mushrooms, quartered

2 cups dry red wine
2 cups gluten-free beef broth
2 teaspoons Italian seasoning
2 cloves garlic, minced
Mashed potatoes or polenta

1. Coat inside of **CROCK-POT®** slow cooker with nonstick cooking spray. Season short ribs with salt and pepper. Heat 1 tablespoon oil in large skillet over medium-high heat. Add ribs in batches; cook 5 to 7 minutes or until browned on all sides, adding additional oil as needed. Transfer to **CROCK-POT®** slow cooker.

2. Return skillet to heat. Add onions; cook and stir 3 minutes or until translucent. Stir in mushrooms, wine, broth, Italian seasoning and garlic; bring to a simmer. Simmer 3 minutes; pour over short ribs. Cover; cook on LOW 10 to 12 hours or on HIGH 6 to 8 hours. Remove ribs and mushrooms to serving platter. Strain cooking liquid. Serve ribs with mashed potatoes and cooking liquid.

Makes 4 to 6 servings

Asian Beef with Mandarin Oranges

2 tablespoons vegetable oil

2 pounds boneless beef chuck roast, cut into ½-inch strips

1 onion, thinly sliced

1 head bok choy, chopped

1 green bell pepper, sliced

1 can (5 ounces) sliced water chestnuts, drained

1 package (about 3 ounces) shiitake mushrooms, sliced

⅓ cup gluten-free soy sauce

2 teaspoons minced fresh ginger

¼ teaspoon salt

1 can (11 ounces) mandarin oranges, drained and syrup reserved

2 tablespoons cornstarch

2 cups gluten-free beef broth

Hot cooked rice

1. Heat oil in large skillet over medium-high heat. Add beef in batches; cook and stir 5 to 7 minutes until browned on all sides. Transfer to **CROCK-POT®** slow cooker.

2. Add onion; cook and stir over medium heat until softened. Add bok choy, bell pepper, water chestnuts, mushrooms, soy sauce, ginger and salt; cook and stir 5 minutes or until bok choy is wilted. Transfer to **CROCK-POT®** slow cooker.

3. Stir reserved mandarin orange syrup into cornstarch in medium bowl until smooth. Whisk into broth in large bowl; pour into **CROCK-POT®** slow cooker. Cover; cook on LOW 10 hours or on HIGH 5 to 6 hours. Stir in mandarin oranges. Serve over rice.

Makes 6 servings

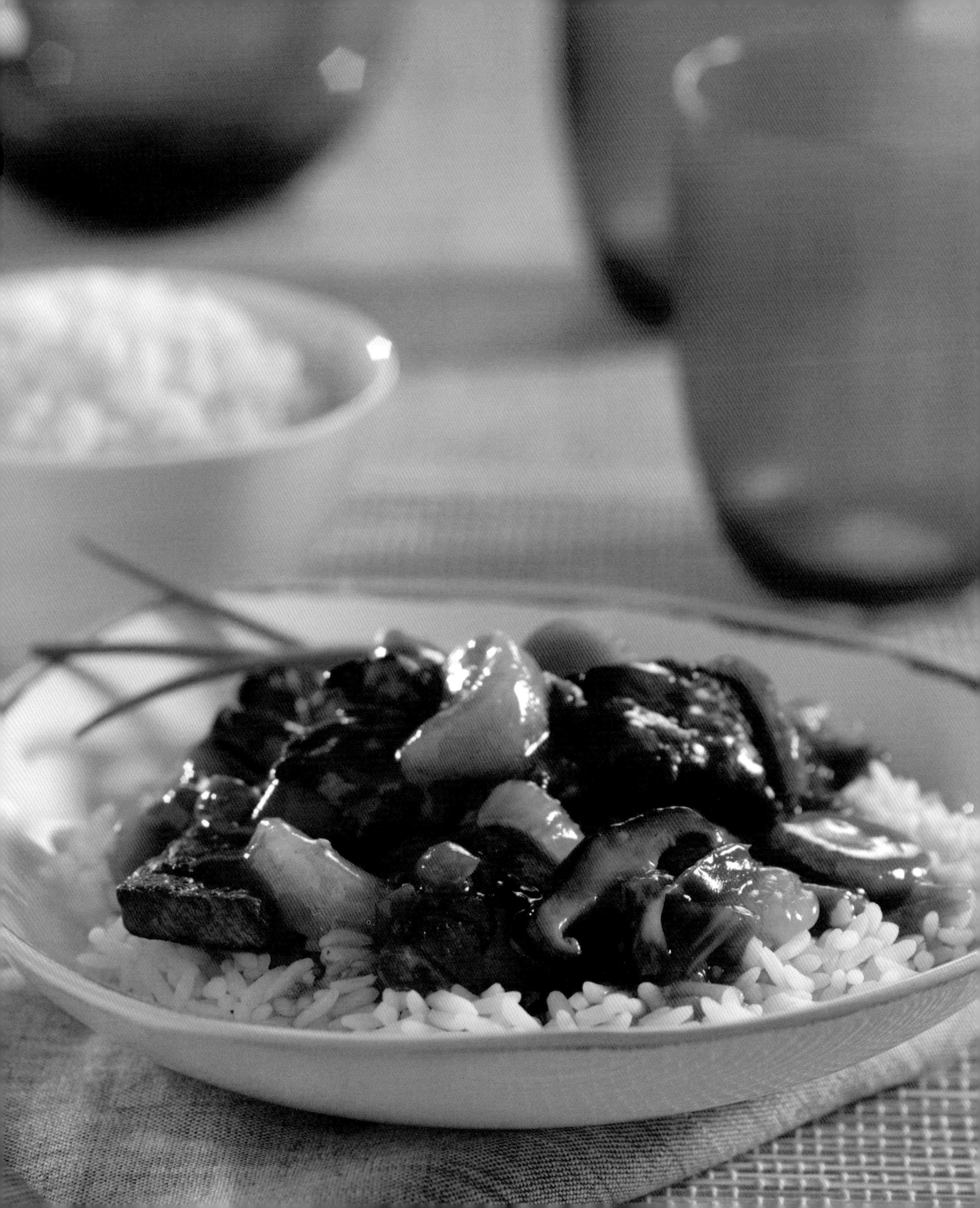

Ginger Beef with Peppers and Mushrooms

1½ pounds boneless beef top round steak, cut into ¾-inch cubes

24 baby carrots

1 onion, chopped

1 red bell pepper, chopped

1 green bell pepper, chopped

1 package (8 ounces) mushrooms, cut into halves

1 cup gluten-free beef broth

½ cup gluten-free hoisin sauce

¼ cup quick-cooking tapioca

2 tablespoons grated fresh ginger

Hot cooked rice

Combine beef, carrots, onion, peppers, mushrooms, broth, hoisin sauce, tapioca and ginger in **CROCK-POT®** slow cooker. Cover; cook on LOW 8 to 9 hours. Serve over rice.

Makes 6 servings

Note: Boneless beef top round steak can also be found in the meat section packaged as London Broil. Both are the same cut of beef, however, London Broil is a thicker cut.

Italian-Style Pot Roast

2 teaspoons minced garlic

1 teaspoon salt

1 teaspoon dried basil

1 teaspoon dried oregano

¼ teaspoon red pepper flakes

1 boneless beef bottom round rump roast or chuck shoulder roast (about 2½ to 3 pounds)*

1 large onion, quartered and thinly sliced

1½ cups tomato-basil or marinara pasta sauce

2 cans (about 15 ounces *each*) cannellini or Great Northern beans, rinsed and drained

¼ cup shredded fresh basil (optional)

*Unless you have a 5-, 6- or 7-quart **CROCK-POT**® slow cooker, cut any roast larger than 2½ pounds in half so it cooks completely.*

1. Combine garlic, salt, dried basil, oregano and red pepper flakes in small bowl; rub over roast.

2. Place onion slices in **CROCK-POT**® slow cooker. Place roast over onion slices. Pour pasta sauce over roast. Cover; cook on LOW 8 to 9 hours.

3. Remove roast to cutting board. Cover loosely with foil; let stand 10 to 15 minutes. Turn off heat. Let liquid in **CROCK-POT**® slow cooker stand 5 minutes. Skim off fat.

4. Turn **CROCK-POT**® slow cooker to LOW. Stir beans into liquid. Cover; cook on LOW 15 to 30 minutes or until beans are heated through. Slice roast across the grain into thin slices. Serve with bean mixture. Garnish with fresh basil.

Makes 6 to 8 servings

Braised Chipotle Beef

3 pounds beef chuck roast, cut into 2-inch pieces

1½ teaspoons salt, plus additional for seasoning

½ teaspoon black pepper, plus additional for seasoning

3 tablespoons vegetable oil, divided

1 large onion, cut into 1-inch pieces

2 red bell peppers, cut into 1-inch pieces

3 tablespoons tomato paste

1 tablespoon minced garlic

1 tablespoon chipotle chili powder*

1 tablespoon paprika

1 tablespoon ground cumin

1 teaspoon dried oregano

1 cup gluten-free beef broth

1 can (about 14 ounces) diced tomatoes

Hot cooked rice

You may substitute regular chili powder.

1. Season beef with salt and black pepper. Heat 2 tablespoons oil in large skillet over medium-high heat. Add beef in batches; cook 5 to 7 minutes until browned on all sides. Transfer each batch to **CROCK-POT**® slow cooker.

2. Return skillet to heat. Add remaining 1 tablespoon oil. Add onion; cook and stir 2 to 3 minutes or just until softened. Add bell peppers; cook 2 minutes. Stir in tomato paste, garlic, chili powder, paprika, cumin, 1½ teaspoons salt, oregano and ½ teaspoon black pepper; cook and stir 1 minute. Transfer to **CROCK-POT**® slow cooker.

3. Return skillet to heat. Add broth; cook and stir to scrape up any browned bits. Pour over beef in **CROCK-POT**® slow cooker. Stir in tomatoes. Cover; cook on LOW 7 hours. Skim fat from sauce. Serve over rice.

Makes 4 to 6 servings

Korean Barbecue Beef

4 to 4½ pounds beef short ribs

¼ cup chopped green onions

¼ cup gluten-free tamari or soy sauce

¼ cup gluten-free beef broth or water

1 tablespoon packed brown sugar

2 teaspoons minced fresh ginger

2 teaspoons minced garlic

½ teaspoon black pepper

2 teaspoons dark sesame oil

Hot cooked rice

2 teaspoons sesame seeds, toasted*

To toast sesame seeds, spread in small skillet. Shake skillet over medium-low heat 2 minutes or until seeds begin to pop and turn golden brown.

1. Place ribs in **CROCK-POT®** slow cooker. Combine green onions, tamari sauce, broth, brown sugar, ginger, garlic and pepper in medium bowl; pour over ribs. Cover; cook on LOW 7 to 8 hours.

2. Remove ribs from cooking liquid. Cool slightly. Trim excess fat and discard. Cut rib meat into bite-size pieces, discarding bones. Turn off heat. Let cooking liquid stand 5 minutes. Skim off fat. Stir oil into cooking liquid.

3. Return beef to **CROCK-POT®** slow cooker. Cover; cook on LOW 15 to 30 minutes or until heated through. Serve over rice; sprinkle with sesame seeds.

Makes 6 servings

Gluten-Free Tip: Tamari is a particular kind of Japanese soy sauce. Some tamari does contain wheat, however, there is a major brand that offers a certified gluten-free, wheat-free tamari. Another option is to substitute a liquid amino concentrate available at health food stores. Bottom line is always check the label!

Thai Steak Salad

- ¼ cup gluten-free soy sauce
- 5 cloves garlic, minced and divided
- 3 tablespoons honey
- 1 pound boneless beef chuck steak, about ¾ inch thick
- ¼ cup gluten-free hoisin sauce
- 2 tablespoons creamy peanut butter
- ½ cup water
- 1 tablespoon minced fresh ginger
- 1 tablespoon ketchup or tomato paste
- 2 teaspoons lime juice
- 1 teaspoon sugar
- ¼ teaspoon gluten-free hot chili sauce or sriracha*
- ½ head savoy cabbage, shredded
- 1 bag (10 ounces) romaine lettuce with carrots and red cabbage
- 1 cup fresh cilantro
- ¾ cup chopped mango
- ½ cup chopped peanuts
- Fresh lime wedges

Sriracha is a Thai hot sauce available in Asian specialty markets. It is sometimes called "rooster sauce," because of the label on the bottle.

1. Coat **CROCK-POT®** slow cooker with nonstick cooking spray. Combine soy sauce, 3 cloves minced garlic and honey in **CROCK-POT®** slow cooker. Add steak; turn to coat. Cover; cook on HIGH 3 hours.

2. Remove steak to cutting board. Cover loosely with foil; let stand 10 to 15 minutes. Slice against the grain into ¼-inch strips.

3. Combine hoisin sauce and peanut butter in medium bowl until smooth. Add water, remaining 2 cloves minced garlic, ginger, ketchup, lime juice, sugar and chili sauce; mix until well blended. Toss cabbage and romaine salad mix with hoisin dressing in large bowl. Top with reserved steak. Sprinkle with cilantro, mango and peanuts. Serve with lime wedges.

Makes 4 to 6 servings

Tip: **CROCK-POT®** slow cookers cook at a low heat for a long time, making them perfect for dishes calling for less-tender cuts of meat.

Sauvignon Blanc Beef with Beets and Thyme

1 pound red or yellow beets, quartered

2 tablespoons extra virgin olive oil

1 beef chuck roast (about 3 pounds)*

1 medium yellow onion, quartered

2 cloves garlic, minced

5 sprigs fresh thyme, plus additional for garnish

1 whole bay leaf

2 whole cloves

1 cup gluten-free chicken broth

1 cup Sauvignon Blanc or dry white wine

2 tablespoons tomato paste

Salt and black pepper

*Unless you have a 5-, 6- or 7-quart **CROCK-POT**® slow cooker, cut any roast larger than 2½ pounds in half so it cooks completely.*

1. Layer beets evenly in **CROCK-POT**® slow cooker. Heat oil in large skillet over medium heat. Add roast; cook 4 to 5 minutes on all sides until browned. Add onion and garlic during last few minutes of cooking. Transfer to **CROCK-POT**® slow cooker.

2. Add 5 sprigs thyme, bay leaf and cloves to **CROCK-POT**® slow cooker. Combine broth, wine, tomato paste, salt and black pepper in medium bowl; stir to combine. Pour over roast and beets in **CROCK-POT**® slow cooker. Cover; cook on LOW 8 to 10 hours. Remove and discard bay leaf and cloves. Garnish with additional thyme sprigs.

Makes 6 servings

Corned Beef and Cabbage

2 onions, thickly sliced

1 corned beef brisket (about 3 pounds) with seasoning packet*

1 package (8 to 10 ounces) baby carrots

6 medium potatoes, cut into wedges

1 cup water

3 to 5 slices bacon

1 head green cabbage, cut into 6 wedges

*Unless you have a 5-, 6- or 7-quart **CROCK-POT**® slow cooker, cut any roast larger than 2½ pounds in half so it cooks completely.*

1. Layer onion slices in **CROCK-POT**® slow cooker. Add corned beef with seasoning packet, carrots and potato wedges. Pour water over top. Cover; cook on LOW 10 hours.

2. Heat large saucepan over medium heat, during last 40 minutes of slow cooking. Add bacon; cook and stir until crisp. Remove to paper towel-lined plate using slotted spoon. Reserve drippings in saucepan. Crumble bacon when cool enough to handle.

3. Place cabbage in saucepan with bacon drippings; cover with water. Bring to a boil; cook 20 to 30 minutes or until cabbage in tender. Drain. Serve corned beef with vegetables. Top with crumbled bacon.

Makes 6 servings

Yankee Pot Roast and Vegetables

1 beef chuck roast (about 2½ pounds), trimmed and cut into bite-size pieces

Salt and black pepper

3 medium baking potatoes (about 1 pound), unpeeled and cut into quarters

2 large carrots, cut into ¾-inch slices

2 stalks celery, cut into ¾-inch slices

1 medium onion, sliced

1 large parsnip, cut into ¾-inch slices

2 whole bay leaves

1 teaspoon dried rosemary

½ teaspoon dried thyme

½ cup gluten-free beef broth

Sprigs fresh basil (optional)

Season beef with salt and pepper. Combine potatoes, carrots, celery, onion, parsnip, bay leaves, rosemary and thyme in **CROCK-POT®** slow cooker. Place beef over vegetables. Pour broth over beef. Cover; cook on LOW 8½ to 9 hours. Remove and discard bay leaves. Remove beef and vegetables to serving platter with slotted spoon. Top with fresh basil.

Makes 10 to 12 servings

Sweet Treats

Cinnamon Latté

6 cups double-strength brewed coffee*

2 cups half-and-half

1 cup sugar

1 teaspoon vanilla

3 cinnamon sticks, plus additional for serving

Whipped cream (optional)

Double the amount of coffee grounds normally used to brew coffee. Or substitute 8 teaspoons instant coffee dissolved in 6 cups boiling water.

Blend coffee, half-and-half, sugar and vanilla in 3- to 4-quart **CROCK-POT®** slow cooker. Add 3 cinnamon sticks. Cover; cook on HIGH 3 hours. Remove and discard cinnamon sticks. Serve latté in tall coffee mugs. Serve with additional cinnamon sticks and whipped cream, if desired.

Makes 6 to 8 servings

Bittersweet Chocolate-Espresso Crème Brûlée

½ **cup chopped gluten-free bittersweet chocolate**

5 **egg yolks**

1¾ **cups heavy cream**

½ **cup granulated sugar**

¼ **cup espresso**

¼ **cup Demerara or raw sugar**

1. Arrange 5 (6-ounce) ramekins or custard cups inside **CROCK-POT®** slow cooker. Pour enough water to come halfway up sides of ramekins (taking care to keep water out of ramekins). Divide chocolate among ramekins.

2. Whisk egg yolks in small bowl; set aside. Place cream, granulated sugar and espresso in small saucepan over medium heat; cook and stir until mixture begins to boil. Pour hot cream mixture in thin, steady stream into egg yolks, whisking constantly. Pour through fine mesh strainer into clean bowl.

3. Ladle into prepared ramekins in bottom of **CROCK-POT®** slow cooker. Cover; cook on HIGH 1 to 2 hours or until custard is set around edges but still soft in centers. Carefully remove ramekins; cool to room temperature. Cover and refrigerate until serving. Spread tops of custards with Demerara sugar. Serve immediately.

Makes 5 servings

Triple Delicious Hot Chocolate

3 cups milk, divided

⅓ cup sugar

¼ cup unsweetened cocoa powder

¼ teaspoon salt

¾ teaspoon vanilla

1 cup whipping cream

1 square (1 ounce) gluten-free bittersweet chocolate, chopped

1 square (1 ounce) gluten-free white chocolate, chopped

Whipped cream

6 teaspoons gluten-free mini semisweet chocolate chips or shaved gluten-free bittersweet chocolate

1. Combine ½ cup milk, sugar, cocoa and salt in **CROCK-POT**® slow cooker; whisk until smooth. Stir in remaining 2½ cups milk and vanilla. Cover; cook on LOW 2 hours.

2. Stir in cream. Cover; cook on LOW 10 minutes. Stir in bittersweet and white chocolate until melted. Pour hot chocolate into mugs. Top each serving evenly with whipped cream and chocolate chips.

Makes 6 servings

Coconut Rice Pudding

2 cups water

1 cup uncooked converted long grain rice

1 tablespoon unsalted butter
   Pinch salt

2¼ cups evaporated milk

1 can (14 ounces) cream of coconut

½ cup golden raisins

3 egg yolks, beaten
   Grated peel of 2 limes

1 teaspoon vanilla
   Toasted shredded coconut (optional)*

To toast coconut, spread in thin layer in heavy-bottomed skillet. Cook and stir over medium heat 2 to 3 minutes or until coconut turns golden. Immediately remove from skillet.

1. Place water, rice, butter and salt in medium saucepan. Bring to a boil over high heat, stirring frequently. Reduce heat to low. Cover; cook 10 to 12 minutes. Remove from heat. Let stand, covered, 5 minutes.

2. Meanwhile, coat inside of **CROCK-POT®** slow cooker with nonstick cooking spray. Add evaporated milk, cream of coconut, raisins, egg yolks, lime peel and vanilla; mix well. Add rice; stir until blended.

3. Cover; cook on LOW 4 hours or on HIGH 2 hours, stirring every 30 minutes. Pudding will thicken as it cools. Garnish with coconut.

Makes 6 servings

Pineapple Daiquiri Sundae Topping

1 pineapple, peeled, cored and cut into ½-inch pieces*

½ cup sugar

½ cup dark rum

3 tablespoons lime juice

Peel of 2 limes, cut into long strips

1 tablespoon cornstarch

Vanilla ice cream

Fresh raspberries and fresh mint leaves (optional)

*You may substitute 1 can (20 ounces) crushed pineapple, drained.

Place pineapple, sugar, rum, lime juice, lime peel and cornstarch in 1½-quart **CROCK-POT®** slow cooker; mix well. Cover; cook on HIGH 3 to 4 hours. Serve over ice cream. Garnish with raspberries and mint.

Makes 4 to 6 servings

Cran-Apple Orange Conserve

2 medium oranges

5 large tart apples, peeled, cored and chopped

2 cups sugar

1½ cups fresh cranberries

1 tablespoon grated lemon peel

1. Remove thin slice from both ends of oranges for easier chopping. Finely chop unpeeled oranges (remove any seeds) to yield about 2 cups chopped oranges.

2. Combine chopped oranges, apples, sugar, cranberries and lemon peel in **CROCK-POT®** slow cooker. Cover; cook on LOW 4 hours or on HIGH 2 hours.

3. Slightly crush fruit with potato masher. Cook, uncovered, on LOW 2 hours or on HIGH 1 to 1½ hours or until thickened, stirring occasionally. Turn off heat. Cool at least 2 hours. Serve over roast pork or poultry.

Makes about 5 cups

Pineapple Daiquiri Sundae Topping

Red Hot Applesauce

10 to 12 apples, peeled, cored and chopped

¾ cup hot cinnamon candies

½ cup apple juice or water

Combine apples, candies and apple juice in **CROCK-POT®** slow cooker. Cover; cook on LOW 7 to 8 hours or on HIGH 4 hours.

Makes 6 servings

Hawaiian Fruit Compote

3 cups coarsely chopped fresh pineapple

3 grapefruits, peeled and sectioned

1 can (21 ounces) cherry pie filling

2 cups chopped fresh peaches

2 to 3 limes, peeled and sectioned

1 mango, peeled and chopped

2 bananas, sliced

1 tablespoon lemon juice

Slivered almonds (optional)

Place pineapple, grapefruits, cherry pie filling, peaches, limes, mango, bananas and lemon juice in **CROCK-POT®** slow cooker; toss lightly. Cover; cook on LOW 4 to 5 hours or on HIGH 2 to 3 hours. Serve with almonds, if desired.

Makes 6 to 8 servings

Serving Suggestion: This sauce is delicious served over roasted turkey, pork roast or baked ham.

Red Hot
Applesauce

Triple Chocolate Fantasy

2 pounds gluten-free vanilla-flavored almond bark, broken into pieces

1 bar (4 ounces) gluten-free chocolate, broken into pieces*

1 package (12 ounces) gluten-free semisweet chocolate chips

3 cups lightly toasted, coarsely chopped pecans**

*Use your favorite high-quality gluten-free chocolate candy bar.

**To toast pecans, spread in single layer in heavy skillet. Cook and stir over medium heat 1 to 2 minutes or until nuts are lightly browned.

1. Place bark, chocolate and chocolate chips in **CROCK-POT®** slow cooker. Cover; cook on HIGH 1 hour. Do not stir.

2. Turn **CROCK-POT®** slow cooker to LOW. Cover; cook on LOW 1 hour, stirring every 15 minutes. Stir in nuts.

3. Drop mixture by tablespoonfuls onto baking sheet covered with waxed paper; let cool. Store in tightly covered container.

Makes 36 pieces

Variations: Here are a few ideas for other imaginative items to add in along with or instead of the pecans: raisins, crushed peppermint candy, crushed toffee, peanuts or pistachio nuts, chopped gum drops, chopped dried fruit, candied cherries, chopped marshmallows or sweetened coconut.

Fresh Bosc Pear Granita

1 pound fresh Bosc pears, peeled, cored and cubed

1¼ cups water

¼ cup sugar

½ teaspoon ground cinnamon

1 tablespoon lemon juice

1. Place pears, water, sugar and cinnamon in **CROCK-POT®** slow cooker. Cover; cook on HIGH 2½ to 3½ hours or until pears are very soft and tender. Stir in lemon juice.

2. Transfer pears and syrup to blender or food processor; blend until smooth. Strain mixture, discarding any pulp. Pour liquid into 11×9-inch baking pan. Cover tightly with plastic wrap. Place pan in freezer.

3. Stir every hour, tossing granita with fork. Crush any lumps in mixture as it freezes. Freeze 3 to 4 hours or until firm. You may keep granita in freezer up to 2 days before serving; toss every 6 to 12 hours.

Makes 6 servings

Fresh Berry Compote

2 cups fresh blueberries	**2 tablespoons orange juice**
4 cups fresh sliced strawberries	**1 cinnamon stick** *or* **½ teaspoon ground cinnamon**
½ cup sugar plus additional as necessary	
4 slices (½ × 1½ inches) lemon peel with no white pith	

1. Place blueberries in **CROCK-POT®** slow cooker. Cover; cook on HIGH 45 minutes or until blueberries begin to soften.

2. Add strawberries, ½ cup sugar, lemon peel, orange juice and cinnamon stick; stir to blend. Cover; cook on HIGH 1 to 1½ hours or until strawberries soften and sugar dissolves. Add additional sugar if necessary; cook until sugar dissolves. Remove stoneware from **CROCK-POT®** slow cooker to heatproof surface; let cool.

Makes 4 servings

Tip: To turn this compote into a fresh fruit topping for ice cream, carefully spoon out fruit. Stir 1 to 2 tablespoons cornstarch into ¼ cup cold water in small bowl until smooth. Whisk into cooking liquid in **CROCK-POT®** slow cooker. Cover; cook on HIGH 10 to 15 minutes or until thickened. Return fruit to sauce; stir gently.

Cherry Rice Pudding

1½ cups milk
1 cup hot cooked rice
3 eggs, beaten
½ cup sugar
¼ cup dried cherries or cranberries

½ teaspoon almond extract
¼ teaspoon salt
Butter
1 cup water
Ground nutmeg (optional)

1. Spray 1½-quart casserole dish that fits in **CROCK-POT®** slow cooker with nonstick cooking spray. Combine milk, rice, eggs, sugar, cherries, almond extract and salt in large bowl; pour into prepared casserole. Cover dish with buttered foil, butter side down.

2. Place rack in **CROCK-POT®** slow cooker; pour in water. Place casserole on rack. Cover; cook on LOW 4 to 5 hours. Remove casserole from **CROCK-POT®** slow cooker. Let stand 15 minutes. Garnish with nutmeg.

Makes 6 servings

Variation: Try substituting 2 tablespoons *each* cherries and cranberries for a delicious new dish.

Mulled Cranberry Tea

2 tea bags

1 cup boiling water

1 bottle (48 ounces) cranberry juice

½ cup dried cranberries (optional)

⅓ cup sugar

1 lemon, cut into ¼-inch slices plus additional for serving

4 cinnamon sticks plus additional for serving

6 whole cloves

1. Place tea bags in **CROCK-POT®** slow cooker. Pour boiling water over tea bags; cover and let steep 5 minutes. Remove and discard tea bags.

2. Stir in cranberry juice, cranberries, if desired, sugar, 1 sliced lemon, 4 cinnamon sticks and cloves. Cover; cook on LOW 2 to 3 hours or on HIGH 1 to 2 hours.

3. Remove and discard cooked lemon slices, cinnamon sticks and cloves. Serve in warm mugs with additional cinnamon sticks and fresh lemon slices.

Makes 8 servings

Tip: The flavor and aroma of ground herbs and spices may lessen during a longer cooking time. So, for slow cooking in your **CROCK-POT®** slow cooker, you may use whole herbs and spices. Just be sure to taste and adjust seasonings before serving.

Pineapple Rice Pudding

1 can (20 ounces) crushed pineapple in juice, undrained

1 can (13½ ounces) unsweetened coconut milk

1 can (12 ounces) evaporated milk

¾ cup uncooked Arborio rice

2 eggs, lightly beaten

¼ cup granulated sugar

¼ cup packed brown sugar

½ teaspoon ground cinnamon

¼ teaspoon salt

¼ teaspoon ground nutmeg

Toasted coconut (optional)*

Fresh pineapple slices (optional)

To toast coconut, spread in thin layer in heavy-bottomed skillet. Cook and stir over medium heat 2 to 3 minutes or until coconut turns golden. Immediately remove from skillet.

Combine pineapple, coconut milk, evaporated milk, rice, eggs, granulated sugar, brown sugar, cinnamon, salt and nutmeg in **CROCK-POT®** slow cooker; mix well. Cover; cook on HIGH 3 to 4 hours or until thickened and rice is tender. Stir until blended. Serve warm or chilled. Garnish with coconut and pineapple slices.

Makes 8 servings

Warm and Spicy Fruit Punch

4 cinnamon sticks

1 orange

1 square (8 inches) double-thickness cheesecloth

1 teaspoon whole allspice

½ teaspoon whole cloves

7 cups water

1 can (12 ounces) frozen cran-raspberry juice concentrate, thawed

1 can (6 ounces) frozen lemonade concentrate, thawed

2 cans (5½ ounces each) apricot nectar

1. Break cinnamon into pieces. Remove strips of orange peel with vegetable peeler or paring knife. Squeeze juice from orange; set juice aside.

2. Rinse cheesecloth; squeeze out water. Wrap cinnamon sticks, orange peel, allspice and cloves in cheesecloth. Tie bag securely with cotton string or strip of cheesecloth.

3. Combine reserved orange juice, water, juice concentrates and apricot nectar in **CROCK-POT®** slow cooker; add spice bag. Cover; cook on LOW 5 to 6 hours. Remove and discard spice bag.

Makes about 14 servings

Tip: To keep punch warm during a party, place your **CROCK-POT®** slow cooker on the buffet table and turn the setting to LOW or WARM.

Chai Tea Cherries 'n' Cream

2 cans (15½ ounces *each*) pitted cherries in pear juice

2 cups water

½ cup orange juice

1 cup sugar

4 cardamom pods

2 cinnamon sticks (broken in half)

1 teaspoon grated orange peel

¼ ounce coarsely chopped candied ginger

4 whole cloves

2 whole black peppercorns

4 green tea bags

1 container (6 ounces) black cherry yogurt

1 quart vanilla ice cream

Sprigs fresh mint (optional)

1. Drain cherries, reserving juice. Set cherries aside. Combine reserved juice, water and orange juice in **CROCK-POT®** slow cooker. Mix in sugar, cardamom pods, cinnamon sticks, orange peel, ginger, cloves and peppercorns. Cover; cook on HIGH 1¾ hours.

2. Remove spices with slotted spoon and discard. Stir in tea bags and reserved cherries. Cover; cook on HIGH 30 minutes.

3. Turn off heat. Remove and discard tea bags. Remove cherries from liquid; set aside. Let liquid cool just until warm. Whisk in yogurt until smooth. Divide warm cherries and yogurt sauce among glasses. Top each serving with ice cream; swirl lightly. Garnish with mint.

Makes 8 servings

Hot Mulled Cider

½ gallon apple cider

½ cup packed brown sugar

1½ teaspoons balsamic or cider vinegar (optional)

1 teaspoon vanilla

1 cinnamon stick

6 whole cloves

½ cup applejack or bourbon (optional)

Combine cider, brown sugar, vinegar, if desired, vanilla, cinnamon stick and cloves in **CROCK-POT®** slow cooker. Cover; cook on LOW 5 to 6 hours. Remove and discard cinnamon stick and cloves. Stir in applejack just before serving, if desired. Serve warm in mugs.

Makes 16 servings

Tip: Cinnamon sticks are used for flavoring hot beverages. Ground cinnamon in boiling or simmering liquid will clump and cause a gritty texture.

Hot Tropics Sipper

4 cups pineapple juice

2 cups apple juice

1 container (about 11 ounces) apricot nectar

½ cup packed dark brown sugar

1 medium orange, thinly sliced plus additional for serving

1 medium lemon, thinly sliced plus additional for serving

3 whole cinnamon sticks

6 whole cloves

Combine pineapple juice, apple juice, nectar, brown sugar, orange slices, lemon slices, cinnamon sticks and cloves in **CROCK-POT®** slow cooker. Cover; cook on HIGH 3½ to 4 hours. Strain immediately. Remove and discard cinnamon sticks. Serve with additional fresh orange and lemon slices, if desired.

Makes 8 servings

Recipe Index

Northwest Beef and
Vegetable Soup (p. 12)

Recipe Index

Recipe Index

Asian Beef Stew (*p. 20*)

Pesto Rice and Beans (*p. 174*)

Recipe Index

Sweet Potato Stew (p. 38)

Supper Squash Medley (p. 166)

**Wild Rice and Dried
Cherry Risotto (*p. 148*)**

Metric Conversion Chart

VOLUME MEASUREMENTS (dry)

1/8 teaspoon = 0.5 mL
1/4 teaspoon = 1 mL
1/2 teaspoon = 2 mL
3/4 teaspoon = 4 mL
1 teaspoon = 5 mL
1 tablespoon = 15 mL
2 tablespoons = 30 mL
1/4 cup = 60 mL
1/3 cup = 75 mL
1/2 cup = 125 mL
2/3 cup = 150 mL
3/4 cup = 175 mL
1 cup = 250 mL
2 cups = 1 pint = 500 mL
3 cups = 750 mL
4 cups = 1 quart = 1 L

VOLUME MEASUREMENTS (fluid)

1 fluid ounce (2 tablespoons) = 30 mL
4 fluid ounces (1/2 cup) = 125 mL
8 fluid ounces (1 cup) = 250 mL
12 fluid ounces (1 1/2 cups) = 375 mL
16 fluid ounces (2 cups) = 500 mL

WEIGHTS (mass)

1/2 ounce = 15 g
1 ounce = 30 g
3 ounces = 90 g
4 ounces = 120 g
8 ounces = 225 g
10 ounces = 285 g
12 ounces = 360 g
16 ounces = 1 pound = 450 g

DIMENSIONS

1/16 inch = 2 mm
1/8 inch = 3 mm
1/4 inch = 6 mm
1/2 inch = 1.5 cm
3/4 inch = 2 cm
1 inch = 2.5 cm

OVEN TEMPERATURES

250°F = 120°C
275°F = 140°C
300°F = 150°C
325°F = 160°C
350°F = 180°C
375°F = 190°C
400°F = 200°C
425°F = 220°C
450°F = 230°C

BAKING PAN AND DISH EQUIVALENTS

Utensil	Size in Inches	Size in Centimeters	Volume	Metric Volume
Baking or Cake Pan (square or rectangular)	8×8×2	20×20×5	8 cups	2 L
	9×9×2	23×23×5	10 cups	2.5 L
	13×9×2	33×23×5	12 cups	3 L
Loaf Pan	8½×4½×2½	21×11×6	6 cups	1.5 L
	9×9×3	23×13×7	8 cups	2 L
Round Layer Cake Pan	8×1½	20×4	4 cups	1 L
	9×1½	23×4	5 cups	1.25 L
Pie Plate	8×1½	20×4	4 cups	1 L
	9×1½	23×4	5 cups	1.25 L
Baking Dish or Casserole			1 quart/4 cups	1 L
			1½ quart/6 cups	1.5 L
			2 quart/8 cups	2 L
			3 quart/12 cups	3 L